So Damn Evil

Geraldine Page

Published by Trellis Publishing, 2021.

While every precaution has been taken in the preparation of this book, the publisher assumes no responsibility for errors or omissions, or for damages resulting from the use of the information contained herein.

SO DAMN EVIL

First edition. July 1, 2021.

Copyright © 2021 Geraldine Page.

ISBN: 979-8224451708

Written by Geraldine Page.

SO DAMN EVIL

GERALDINE PAGE

KERRY DALTON

Louise Melanie "Louise" May was looking for a place to stay.

She had three children but had them taken away as the courts declared her to be an unfit parent because of her drug addiction. At the age of 23, she needed to get her life back together.

Things seemingly could not get any worse for the recovering addict.

But then she arrived at the home of Kerry Dalton seeking help.

"I don't have anywhere to go," Louise said, realizing that her audience in Kerry Lyn Dalton was only half paying attention. "Rob is in jail. They took away my kids. Damn CPS."

The frazzled haired twenty-eight-year-old alternated between staring at the television and smoking on the meth pipe. She took a deep toke on the pipe and let the smoke out.

"You can stay with me," she finally said.

"Oh my God, thank you," Louise said.

"But it is only until Rob gets out," Kerry said.

"I understand. I understand. No problem."

But Louise had a problem. Meth addiction.

Now she had added another problem in Kerry Lyn Dalton.

"Kerry was a queen in the subculture of meth and alcoholism if there is such a thing," forensic psychologist

Greta Smith said. "She had been married twice and had five children by three different men. It was amazing how Kerry Dalton even survived to the age of 28. Unemployable, she was the epitome of a bully and would do anything to get her way. She had little regard for the rights or feelings of other people, running roughshod over everyone in her path."

Unfortunately for Louise, she had gotten in Kerry's way.

Kerry would be arrested for drug possession and hauled off to jail for a short stint. She had been Louise's supplier and Louise needed her fix.

But she had no money.

So she began pawning off things she found around the house during a spur of the moment "garage sales." Some of Kerry's old jewelry would be sold off in exchange for drugs.

But when Kerry was released from prison and found out that her stuff had been pawned off, she became more than livid.

She became homicidal.

"Kerry took the theft as a personal affront," Smith said. "This was a fragile living situation between two drug addicts. Junkies. They had little regard for one another and really see each other as utilities to use or supply drugs. Louise is willing to sell out Kerry's stuff while Kerry is willing to kill Louise to gain revenge."

On June 26th, 1988, Kerry confronted Louise at the mobile home. Three other people in their drug dealing clique soon arrived, Mark Lee Tompkins, Sheryl Baker and another transient named "George".

Kerry ordered Louise to sit down and tied her to a chair. She then began torturing her, splicing off and electrical cord and burning her with it.

Louise screamed in pain.

Tompkins then began joining in the torture, jabbing at the defenseless Louise with a screwdriver.

The two then demanded that Sheryl partake in the abuse as well. Reluctantly, Sheryl complied.

"Sheryl felt as if they would have killed her if she didn't do as she was told," Smith said.

After the course of a few hours, the three then took turns torturing Louise.

Kerry enjoyed shocking her captive with the electric cord, laughing as Louise screamed. Seeking to raise the stakes, her boyfriend took an iron skillet and smashed it against the back of Louise's head.

"They hit her with such force that it made a dent in the pan," Smith said.

Kerry's sadism was still not satiated. She kept thinking of different ways to torture Louise then came up with the idea to inject her with some battery acid. Her boyfriend got a syringe and they plunged the battery acid into her vein as well as poured it down her throat.

"Kerry was a sadist," Smith said. "She justified her torture of Louise to the fact that the woman sold a few items of her jewelry and got maybe twenty-five bucks for it."

Tompkins then put Louise out of her misery by stabbing her in the neck with the screwdriver. She fell to the ground and he began stomping on her head until she died.

What happened to Louise's body after remains shrouded in mystery and hearsay.

Later that evening, a sheriff arrived at the mobile home on a burglary call. He saw no evidence of a burglary but did describe one of the residents, Joann Fedor, as high on meth. The sheriff then inspected the exterior and interior of the mobile home, finding nothing.

The disappearance of Louise remained unsolved for three years until Sheryl Baker had a crisis of conscience. She confessed to the crime, telling the authorities of what happened the day Louise was killed. In return for her confession, the authorities allowed her to plead to second-degree murder.

One of Louise's cousins stated on-line that the prosecuting attorney told her that one of trio involved admitted that they dismembered the body of Louise. They then spread the body parts out across different locations on different Indian reservations.

"For meth heads," Smith said. "They certainly knew what they were doing when disposing of a body. They were all jobless junkies but when it came to murdering someone they were willing to work hard. Damn hard in order to avoid detection. They would have avoided detection but for Sheryl Baker finally coming forward."

Kerry's trial would begin on February 8th, 1995. The judge, Thomas J. Whelan stated that

"I think the record is clear that nobody has ever been found in this case. The record is equally clear that there is circumstantial evidence that there was a homicide. There's also conflicting circumstantial evidence that it may not be a homicide; in fact, she may still be alive ..."

"My reason for making these statements is to establish for the record that in my mind corpus is a legitimate issue in this case. It's not a ruse that - there is a legitimate issue before the jury as to whether or not there's - a corpus of a homicide has been established."

Kerry would never confess to the crime on record and would claim innocence.

"The thing that makes me the most mad is that he is lying, and he knows he's lying," Kerry said of the prosecuting attorney.

The jury foreman, John Castleman, would concede that they found her guilty on the basis of "the type of murder it was" despite a lack of physical evidence to prove that Louise was murdered.

Mark Thompkins would be convicted of first-degree murder.

Kerry Dalton would be sentenced to death on May 23rd, 1995.

"She is the epitome of evil," Smith said. "We can say the drugs did it but there was a lot of premeditation to what she did to poor Louise. If anyone deserves to be on death row and have her execution expedited, it is Kerry Dalton."

Victoria Forbes, however, continues to champion the innocence of her sister.

"She was convicted without a body," Forbes said. "Without a weapon, without any blood evidence, without any physical evidence, without a crime scene, without anyone being declared deceased nearly seven years later as she stood trial with no one declared deceased being charged with the death penalty."

There continued to be some on-line controversy regarding Kerry's guilt as her supporters point to the fact that Louise's husband claims to have had a call from Louise a week after she was murdered.

That "evidence", however, is all they have to go on.

Despite Dalton's persistence at an appeal, it was clear to law officials believe that Kerry Dalton was guilty of the murder of Irene Louise May. Neither Tompkins nor Baker had anything to go after coming forward after three years of silence. They finally sobered up and confessed their crime.

Kerry Dalton did not and is now on death row.

SHEILA THE KILLER

LAURA PENA

PROLOGUE

The farmhouse and surrounding area looked like something from the set of "Little House on the Prairie."

The house on Harvey Farm stood nestled in between tall pine trees, peaceful streams, and wildlife.

A place where you don't expect to find scenes that would be given an "X" rating if it were a horror movie.

The police arrived at the home while conducting a search for a missing young man named Kenneth Countje. They did not have to search far to find evidence of criminal activity. In the front of the property, lay a mattress burning alongside a smoking garbage barrel.

Their first inclination was to believe that the resident was burning garbage. A citation was due, maybe, but they had more pressing matters to attend to.

But upon closer inspection of the barrel, the officers saw a bone sticking out of the garbage.

A femur?

A mass of fleshy goo remained at the knob of the bone and the smell of the charred remains made the policemen gag.

They both gave each other a look of horror. Here in a town where the most serious crime would be a speeding ticket or jaywalking, the police were about to enter a whole world of horror beyond their wildest imagination.

CHAPTER ONE

Epping, New Hampshire.

Population = less than six thousand.

Epping is a rainy, small town that has been sarcastically nicknamed "The Center of the Universe". That has not stopped the residents from hosting parades, canoe races and music festivals. But when Sheila LaBarre arrived, the tiny hamlet soon became known for murder.

"She was a smart woman," forensic psychologist Paula Orange said. "Not book smart but intuitive. She could read people."

Sheila was born Sheila Kaye Bailey in Fort Payne, Alabama in 1958.

She was the youngest of six children. Her first marriage with a man named Ronnie Jennings would last less than two months. Jennings would find out that Sheila had been locking his child from a previous marriage in a closet to punish her. Jennings would divorce Sheila but she would find herself a new man in short order, tying the knot with John Baxter and moving to Chattanooga, Tennessee. Even though married, she would secretly fantasize about being swept away by a rich man. Sheila's mental illness would come to bear in her second marriage and that would end in divorce as well. Despondent, Sheila tried to kill herself and was sent to a psychiatric facility. She would be raped by an orderly inside the hospital.

Now single in Tennessee, the cash-strapped Sheila was forced to live in a local YMCA. She attended a church service and had a private talk with one of the preachers as she wanted "spiritual guidance." She would later claim that the reverend asked if she wanted to "sit in his lap." She then went to a psychiatrist who asked her if she had anal sex with any of her former husbands. The doctor then called Sheila at home and asked if "what she was wearing" and if she "was touching herself."

"If what we are to believe all of Sheila's stories," Orange said. "Then literally all of her interactions with men have ended with them as the pervert and her as the victim. Her sister would later testify that Sheila was molested by her father when she was young. Then her abusive marriages, the rape at the psych facility segues into a spiritual search where she meets a preacher who shows her the tent in his pants. Crazy."

CHAPTER TWO

Sheila turned to personal ads after her failures in marriage. She didn't like the normal courtship process of going to bars and meeting men there. She used the personal ads to cherry pick the men she wanted, men she could dominate.

"Whether on-line or off-line, Sheila behaved like a woman who was in complete control," Orange said. "She would develop a strange kind of power over men. It was almost as if she knew which men would be vulnerable to her feminine wiles and which ones would fight back. But when it came to Dr. Bill LaBarre, it was more of a case of getting the money."

While in Tennessee, Dr. LaBarre decided to take out a personal ad. He would get a response from Sheila who immediately sought to separate herself from the other paramours of the rich doctor.

She sent the doctor nude Polaroids of herself.

The strategy worked.

"She showed no shame in flirting with the older man and soon had him in the palm of her hand," Orange said. "He'd buy her fancy clothes, necklaces, the whole nine yards."

Wilfred "Bill" LaBarre was a successful chiropractor but lonely. Overweight and bespectacled, he had little to offer aside from his wealth. He was in his sixties and recently widowed.

Dr. Labarre was considered a good man by all who knew him. He had been the "Chiropractor of the Year" in 1983 but that would be the same year his beloved Edwina would pass away from cancer. Eager to salve the loneliness, he married another woman named Leona but she abandoned the doctor after a few years. He had two children from his first marriage; Laura and Gregory.

Now alone and widowed, the doctor wanted to spend his golden years enjoying his wealth.

And a young woman.

He would look at the nude Polaroids of the curvaceous Southern Belle, becoming obsessed.

"Here was a lonely, older man who all of a sudden had a 27-year old woman sending him nude photos. He thought he hit the jackpot."

Dr. LaBarre soon invited Sheila to come live with him at his farm in Epping, New Hampshire. The farm was a spacious one, a 115-acre horse ranch that according to LaBarre, "needed a female hand."

Sheila would become enamored by life on the farm, at least at first. She "never heard a June bug before" and the isolated country home gave her a peace that she never experienced.

Neighbors were not shocked that Dr. LaBarre took in such a younger woman as his girlfriend. He reportedly had other girlfriends after his wife died. "Sheila ran all the other girls off," one neighbor said.

But Sheila would prove to be a high-maintenance girlfriend. She would drain Dr. LaBarre's finances, making him buy her gifts and prizes which included a brand-new Silver Mercedes.

She also began to interject herself into LaBarre's estate and business dealings.

The farm that LaBarre owned was called the Old Harvey Farm. It was named after the original owners of the property who still lived in the area. But Sheila forced the doctor to change the name, she wanted it called something that reflected her personality.

The Silver Leopard Farm.

Sheila then had a sign made up and had it placed at the entrance.

She was marking her territory.

CHAPTER THREE

Despite the constant gifts and financial prizes, Sylvia proved to be an ungrateful sugar baby. The relationship would turn tempestuous after a few months. Sheila would claim that Dr. LaBarre often referred to himself as an "old fart" and looked the other way when Sheila began to have different men over for sex.

"He just worried about me when I would date far from home. But he was getting old and his heart would stop beating sometimes."

But the couple fought and police were routinely called to the residence to mediate their domestic disputes.

"You would sometimes hear gunshots," Bruce Allen, a LaBarre neighbor said. "You would hear her screaming, 'I'm going to kill you, you mother fucker!'"

Sheila once pulled a gun on the doctor and forced him out of the home. The chiropractor hid behind a boulder as his girlfriend shot at him.

LaBarre's daughter also recalled that she heard Sheila screaming threats at her father. "I'm gonna kill the horses and I'm going to kill you too."

Laura would later remark at how much her father changed after Sheila came into his life. He went from a normal, well-liked member of the community to a meek, submissive man.

"Sheila was all about being an opportunist," Orange said. "She had the ability to read a man, analyzing his weaknesses, size him up and then push the buttons. With LaBarre, she had a lonely man in front of her. He would tolerate anything in order not to lose her at first and then he simply became fearful of his life. These men in this small New England town did not have the wherewithal to deal with a violent sociopath like Sheila."

Sheila didn't stop with the renaming of Old Harvey Home. She soon took over the accounting duties at LaBarre's chiropractic business. She began organizing the practice into a well-oiled machine. She would track down patients who owed the doctor money and file numerous small claims in the Hampton District Court.

Concerned friends would advise him to dump Sheila before it was too late but it became apparent that the doctor either didn't know how or was afraid to. Dr. LaBarre informed neighbor Bruce Allen that he "had to get rid of her" and that he wanted to "send her back to Alabama. Hopefully, she'll stay there."

Her power over Dr. LaBarre increased to the point where he had given her power of attorney. She began rewriting his will, becoming the executor of his estate. The will stated that he was leaving everything to "a very special lady known as Sheila Kaye Jennings LaBarre."

"The will was very carefully redacted from the original," Orange said. "She kept a lot of the parts of the original and used her own typewriter to amend the little detail of where all the assets will go to. She was very astute and covered her tracks very well for someone who was supposedly schizophrenic."

The two would live together (Sheila would move out briefly but claim to be his common-law wife) from 1987 until LaBarre's death in 2000 at the age of 74. The coroner logged his cause of death as heart disease. There were suspicions among those close to the doctor that believe Sheila poisoned him to hasten the process.

"He was pretty old," Orange said. "And according to the autopsy, the heart disease was significant. So Sheila didn't have anything to do with his death despite the suspicions. The killings would come later."

Sheila would inherit the farm, LaBarre's Chiropractor office, two apartments and a rental home.

This was all valued at over two million dollars in assets.

Strangely, Sheila would marry a Jamaican national named Wayne Ennis in August of 1995 while living with Dr. LaBarre. Ennis drove a tour bus around Jamaica and Sheila made sure that when she toured the islands with Dr. LaBarre that they would cross paths with her Jamaican lover. She arranged for Ennis to obtain a visa and took him back to the farm with her. She would later claim that she and the doctor had stopped having sex and that she "had needs" which apparently Ennis took care of. She would later concede to pleasing the doctor sexually, "I'd use my hand," she said afterward.

Ennis would live in the farmhouse for almost a year. He had his own numerous encounters with Sheila which were violent and bizarre. One night, she ordered him to get in the car. The two then drove around the quiet town, Sheila's voice taking on a conspiratorial tone.

"I wish one of those damn horses would just kick him (Dr. LaBarre) in the head," Sheila said. "Kick him in the head and kill his old ass. I've thought about strangling him myself. But now I have a better idea. I want you to kill him."

Ennis was too frightened to say no to Sheila. The two would eventually divorce and the court records reveal that Sheila took out a restraining order against him.

Ennis disputed the allegations and stated that Sheila was the abuser.

He would later recall being punched, pushed, and shot at by Sheila.

"She told me that she was going to send me back to Jamaica in a box," Ennis said.

Dr. LaBarre told Ennis that Sheila was crazy and believed that she would eventually kill him. He gave the Jamaican money and sent him to the bus station, requesting that he leave town for his own safety.

After the relationship with Ennis ended, Sheila began dating James Brackett.

She and James would remain together for six years despite the fact that Sheila would attack Brackett with a pair of scissors, a machete, and an ax. When all of that failed she tried to shoot him.

The two would break up after which Brackett would get himself a vanity license plate that read "I'm Alive."

Brackett recalled moments where Sheila would act sweet and nice only to go into a violent rage moments later. He said that the greatest example was a time when he was taking a long bath with Sheila only to have her get out of the tub and smash him in the face with a two-foot grill brush.

Two of his teeth would be knocked out from the impact.

Sheila would attack Brackett for a variety of transgressions that would not be guilty of. Hurting her rabbits, damaging her property or having affairs with other women.

Brackett finally had enough, escaping from the farm on one rainy night and hitchhiking back into town.

"I'm lucky to be alive," he would later state.

CHAPTER FOUR

Sheila inherited the farm after LaBarre's death. The doctor's children tried to contest the will but were told that the odds of winning the case were 50/50 at best. They would also have to front over $50,000 to pay for the court costs.

Sheila soon turned the farm into her own private fiefdom. She would hire young men to help her around the place then pay them with her sexual favors or sometimes just beat the shit out of them.

"There would neighbors that would claim to see young men leave her house," Orange said. "They would look beaten up; black eyes, bloody lips, facial contusions. God knows what else."

Her neighbors began to suspect something fishy was going on but had no real evidence to call the police with.

"The first time I met Sheila LaBarre was at the Harvey Farm Stand," said Bonnie Meroth, one of Sheila's neighbors. "It was during the summertime when the produce was ready. I had no basic interaction with her except that of someone standing next to another person as a consumer. And she suddenly turned around and said 'I'll kill you if you come down to my farm' or words to that effect."

Bonnie would later claim that Sheila would try to scare her while driving down the road, nearly running her over while she was on her morning walk.

When she wasn't intimidating neighbors and townsfolk, Sheila would use the farm as the playground for her own private fetishes.

She liked to control and bully men. Stroking one of her pet rabbits, she would punish and insult the men unlucky enough to work at her farm.

"Are you kidding me?" Sheila yelled at the young man who dropped the wheelbarrow. "This should have been done yesterday."

He was young and naive, needing money. If it meant taking lip from Sheila, so be it. He needed work and she seemed nice when she hired him.

"Hurry up!" Sheila said, kicking the man in his buttocks. "Move, move. Are you kidding me? I've never seen a lazier man in my life."

Fatigued after working sixteen hours for seven days straight, the young man keeled over in exhaustion, dropping the wheelbarrow.

"Bitch made, perverted ass pedophile!" Sheila said. "Is this what I am paying you for? I am paying you to work. Now get off your bitch ass. Now!"

It became apparent that Sheila had a gift. A gift of controlling a certain type of man. Verbally abusive and overbearing, she encountered very little resistance.

She kicked the young man again. "Your name is 'bitch', you hear me?"

His real name was Michael Deloge.

CHAPTER FIVE

Deloge had problems as a teen. He got caught up in drugs and found himself on the streets, living out of homeless shelters. In 2004, he would meet Sheila LaBarre.

Deloge became smitten with the woman whom he saw as the life of the party. She would drink beer and play country songs on a guitar. According to Deloge's stepfather, Gordon Boston, the duo would indulge in drugs and study "sadistic material".

Deloge would join Sheila at her farm and soon become her personal whipping boy. Sheila would slap him around like a rag doll. One of the fellow ranch hands, Philip Sullos, recalled witnessing Sheila beating on Deloge with a hardwood stick until he bled. Deloge cowered and took the beating. She would then throw Deloge into a windowless shack and slam the door shut.

Deloge would cower meekly in the corner until Sheila came and got him, making no attempt to escape.

He would be declared missing in 2004 and no one would ever see him again.

In February of 2006, Sheila began looking for a new farmhand. She had her own criteria. He had to be young but pliable to her controlling methods.

She would find the perfect foil in Kenny Countie.

"Kenny was a lovely boy," Carolynn Lodge, Kenny's mother said. "He couldn't do enough for you. Everyone was his friend. I was so proud of him. He never had a horrible word for anybody and that was the problem. He trusted everybody."

Kenny's trust would lead him into Sheila LaBarre's trap.

Kenny would answer one of Sheila's personal ads. The young man was still naive and according to some reports had a "low IQ". The two met through a telephone personal ad service with Sheila calling up the young man and charming him in a way that no woman ever did.

"He (Kenny) told my son Brian that he met a 47-year old woman in New Hampshire," Lodge said. "She owned a farm. She owned a beautiful car. And she was rich. And he was serious about her."

"Kenny fit Sheila's psychological criteria," Orange said. "She targeted men whom she could overpower not only physically but also mentally. She was older than Kenny and light years more cunning. She knows exactly what to say and do to push his buttons. She takes the lead, telling him that he is going to be 'in for the time of his life' and that she 'can't wait to see him.' To a young man with limited experience and intelligence like Kenny, this is music to his ears."

Sheila would arrive at Kenny's home in the silver Mercedes. The silver leopard, the cougar, picking up her prey and taking him back to her lair.

Kenny's family would never see him again.

Sheila would use the same methods on Kenny as she did on the men in the past. She seduced the young man first then isolated him in her farmhouse. Then she berated him verbally before beating the shit out of him with face slaps, punches, and a wooden stick.

The beatings would come to a head during a weekend in February of 2000. Sheila beat Kenny's face into a pulp, took the wooden cane to his legs and may have poisoned him.

Then she decided to take him shopping at Walmart.

Placing him in a wheelchair, she rolled him around the outlet as she stocked up on garden supplies. She dumped two containers of diesel fuel into the prone Kenny's lap.

Little did he know that she would later use the gas to incinerate his body.

Customers gawked at the odd couple, concerned about the contusions on Kenny's face.

"Fuck you looking at?" Sheila would scream as she sped down through the aisle.

Employees of the store soon became concerned, calling the police.

The cops would arrive, confronting the couple in the store. They inquired about Kenny's condition but he didn't respond. Instead, Sheila took the lead, telling Kenny that he "didn't have to talk to these assholes."

The police didn't follow through. Kenny remained silent as Sheila rolled him through the store and out the door. No crime had been witnessed and they let the couple go.

Kenny's mother would later sue the police for negligence but it was tossed out of court in 2010.

A few nights after the Walmart incident, Sheila would make a frantic phone call to the police.

"I got a pervert in my house!" she screamed into the phone. "He's a pedophile! A pedophile!"

In a bizarre sequence of events, Sheila began to play a recording for the detective on the other end. She had routinely audio recorded everything she did, trying to incriminate the young men she worked with into admitting they were pedophiles. On this occasion, she played back a recording of her and Kenny.

"On the tape was my son, vomiting," Lodge said. "He kept saying 'he's faking, he's faking.'"

Sheila would ask Kenny if he was a pedophile on the tape. Kenny would answer 'yes'.

"Now he's a pedophile," Kenny's mother said. "Now he's raping children. Raping his brother. He's vomiting."

The police would write off the call as the rantings of a schizophrenic. They did not immediately respond to the residence.

Sheila would then kill Kenny Countie.

"She had to justify the killing of the young men in her own mind," Orange said. "For some bizarre reason, she would brainwash herself into thinking that her victims were pedophiles. She would repeat the question like a mantra, 'Are you a pedophile? Are you a pedophile?' Working herself up into an angry and violent state of mind before she killed the man."

Sheila's sister, Lynn Noojin, believed that Sheila was sexually abused by her father. Because of this, she became obsessed with child molestation. She would accuse the young men that worked for her of various sexual deviations, including pedophilia, incest, and bestiality.

CHAPTER SIX

After the bizarre call to police, authorities would not arrive at the farmhouse until the next morning. The police would enter the grounds, seeing both the burning mattress and barrel with Kenny's remains. They would not identify the burning bones as belonging to Kenny until much later.

Sheila had murdered Kenny the night before. She attacked Kenny ferociously with a kitchen knife, pushing the already weakened young man to the floor and stabbing away.

Blood sprayed and splattered everywhere.

Sheila then dragged Kenny's body out to her yard where she doused his body with the diesel fuel they had purchased at Walmart.

Lighting a match, she set the dead man on fire. She then took her pet rabbit in her lap, pulled up a chair and watched Kenny Countie burn.

"He was dismembered," Kenny's mother said, fighting tears. "And he was put in a pit and burned. But my son, he just wanted to be loved. I can't imagine what he must have been thinking. Because he was all alone."

Police would look throughout the house and find blood splatter on the walls and floor. A forensic team arrived and matched the blood with Kenny's DNA sample from his Army days. They would find the wallet of Michael Deloge but not his body.

Hundreds of police would spend seventeen days searching the 115-acre property. They found numerous burn pits and blood remains that were so old they had layers of dust on them. They would find clothing that belonged to Deloge and some toes that remain unidentified (it is rumored that the toes may belong to a mysterious Irish man who Sheila claims was stalking her.)

Going on the run from the cops, Sheila hitchhiked along Interstate 293. She was then picked up by Stephen Martello.

"Thanks so much for stopping," Sheila said.

"No problem," Martello said, looking the buxom Southern Belle up and down. His heart began to race.

Will he get lucky?

"My car broke down about two miles back. I got into a fight with my boyfriend and I'm trying to get to Dorchester."

"I'm headed that way," Martello said.

Sheila clutched her purse as if it were a security blanket and she kept looking back at the rear window.

"You all right?" he asked.

"Yeah," Sheila said "Just a little rattled. You know, it has been a tough day."

Martello took Sheila to the drug store when she said she needed to stop off and "buy some things". He tailed Sheila around the store until she bought a douche. Noting her erratic behavior, Martello disappeared out of Sheila's earshot to call the police on his cell phone.

"Hi," Martello said. "Just curious if you folks are looking for someone who just robbed a bank or an escaped mental patient. I just met a woman who is acting kind of strange."

When the authorities informed him that they were not actively investigating someone with that kind of background, Martello took Sheila to a hotel room.

The two would engage in wild and loud sex.

"You just had sex with an angel," Sheila proclaimed after they were done.

"Is that right?"

"You're not like the other men," Sheila said. "My boyfriend, Jesus, I just caught him with a huge stack of child porn. He is a pedophile. So are all those damn cops. Pedophiles, all of them. I think all sex offenders must die."

Martello said nothing. Instead, he put his pants and shoes on as fast as he could as Sheila continued to go on another bizarre rant.

"Vengeance is mine saith the Lord," Sheila said, laying on the bed in post-coital repose. "I was sent back to earth as an angel. I know how to speak to God in Hebrew. Do it every night."

Martello excused himself and high-tailed it out of the hotel room. He arrived home and saw the television broadcast about Sheila. He didn't call the police, worried that he would be an accessory to her crimes. Instead, Martello drove to the station and practically sprinted to the front desk.

"I think I just met Sheila LaBarre."

"To the end, Sheila had control over just about every man put in front of her," Orange said. "Here was a guy who picks her up at the side of the road. He thinks she is crazy enough to where he calls the cops to find out if there are any missing mental patients. He knows that she has a screw loose but he has sex with her anyway. It may be a poor reflection on men for sure but his response is typical. The men that Sheila encountered, from Dr. LaBarre all the way to Stephen Martello, all had the same false narratives going on in their head. They did not see a beautiful woman as something evil. It just didn't fit their narrative. So when Sheila begins her abuse, they just can't believe it. They refuse to hit a 'woman' back. She gets them 'pussy whipped' then beats the shit out of them. Rinse and repeat."

Sheila LaBarre would later be arrested for the murders of Michael Deloge and Kenneth Countje. She would plead no guilty on the grounds of insanity.

"This is a sick, sick woman," her attorney would argue. "Deeply disturbed."

Court-appointed psychiatrists would agree, testifying that Sheila was delusional as well as schizophrenic.

The jury would visit both LaBarre's farm and the Walmart where she frequented first hand. Sheila would join them as well although she was forced to wear a stun belt.

The jury did not buy her insanity defense and found her guilty.

"The fact that she has to remain for the rest of her life behind bars," Kenny's mother said. "She got what she asked for. She'll never see the light of day. Horrible thing is that my son, he's not here with me. He was only twenty-four."

Sheila LaBarre is now serving life in without possibility of parole.

Ruthless : Husband Killer Ruth Snyder

Ana Benson

Ruth Snyder Biography

The Roaring Twenties were a time of great change in the United States. The population in the cities grew rapidly, women were gaining more rights, and the widespread of newspapers allowed everyone to read the latest news from every corner of the country. So if a crime occurred somewhere, millions of people would be able to follow the case as it developed. New York was getting pretty crowded as well and it was the place to be if you wanted to make a name for yourself.

Probably the most iconic symbol of the Twenties was the flapper girl. They were young women who liked to dress well, dance, and party till the early morning hours. But when a flapper girl from New York murdered her husband in order to collect the insurance money, everyone watched the story unfold. So many intriguing details were uncovered immediately after the crime that the majority of readership simply couldn't get enough of the juicy details and ended up following the court proceedings until the very end.

Early life

Ruth Snyder was born sometime in late 1895 to parents who immigrated from Sweden and Norway. Their European family name was Sorenson which Ruth's father changed to Brown when they settled in America. He didn't want a foreign sounding name and wanted his family to both blend in and find work.

Her father worked as a sailor while the family was still in Europe but made a decision to spend more time with his wife and children so he became a carpenter. Ruth's mother would stay at home and take care of her and her older brother.

Taking care of Ruth would prove to be a full-time job as she had many health issues. She suffered from epilepsy and would often have seizures that would make her end up in the doctor's office on a weekly basis. Her appendix was also removed and the procedure itself left a toll on her tiny body. There were probably some mistakes during the operation that damaged her internal organs. She would have unexplainable stomach pains throughout her life thanks to this unfortunate surgical intervention.

Since it was the early 1900s and Browns were working class, they struggled with finances. But this didn't stop Ruth to long for the expensive things. Her parents always felt bad when they had to tell her that they couldn't afford a fancy piece of clothing she had set her eyes upon or a brand new toy. But the poverty didn't have a strong influence on the religious views of the Brown family and they attended church regularly. Ruth would be forced to attend but would later state that she didn't believe in God.

Ruth Snyder wasn't an exceptional student and hated going to school. All she wanted in life was to find a husband who would love her and provide their family everything that she didn't have growing up. She knew that America was a land of opportunities and that there were many bachelors with a work ethic and wealth that she desired.

Ruth would later quit school and find a job at New York Telephone Company as a trainee. The pay wasn't much but it was enough to allow her to support herself until she found a husband that had the qualities she desired. Ruth was tall, blonde, and quite attractive...Deep down, she knew it would only be a matter of time before she found a worthy suitor. She would end up working a graveyard shift for almost two years before she could quit New York Telephone Company. The reason was - she found herself a man. His name was Albert Snyder and he was much older than her. The age difference didn't bother her at first but it became a real problem after a couple of months.

Marriage to Albert Snyder

Prior to his marriage to Ruth Brown, Albert Snyder had a fiancée named Jesse who died before they could tie the knot. He spent years avoiding relationships but felt like he was ready to fall in love once again when he met Ruth. His new romantic interest didn't have Jesse's wit but she seemed desirous upon having a family which was what Albert wanted. A woman who would stay home.

Albert worked as a magazine editor and since he was covering boats and watercrafts, his greatest passion was sailing.

Ruth was completely different from Jesse. She didn't like reading or sailing which did bother Albert sometimes. While Ruth was sure of her love towards Albert, she was constantly reminded of his undying love to the ex-fiancée. His sailboat was called "Jesse" and their family house was decorated with Jesse's portraits. They would often argue about this obsession but Albert didn't want to remove these items.

Despite her jealousy, Ruth refused to leave Albert. As a matter of fact, she got pregnant with their child regardless of the fact that Albert didn't any children. Ruth gave birth to a healthy baby girl they named Lorraine. Albert couldn't hide his disappointment. If he were to have a child, he wanted it to be a boy.

In the end, Ruth was the only one who cared for the infant. Albert wasn't interested at all and would often comment on how Ruth lost her attractiveness after she had given birth. The Snyder family needed a bigger house now that there were three of them so they relocated to Queens Village in 1923. Since Ruth needed someone to help her take care of baby Lorraine, she invited her mother to stay with them.

Visibly disappointed in her husband and his behavior, Ruth was now free to explore New York's nightlife and be more social. She would leave Lorraine with her mother and head out to the night clubs without Albert. She found a new circle of friends who loved going out and having fun. Ruth wasn't secretive and had many lovers during this period of her life. They would meet in hotels but Ruth would sometimes invite them back to her home when she knew Albert was working. She would also spend her time at a nearby Swedish restaurant which served foods she remembered from her childhood. This is here that she met Judd Gray, a corset maker.

This was a fortunate event because Albert did give her many negative remarks about the shape of her post-partum body. Ruth thought a corset could help with her figure so she met with Judd Gray at his boutique. Nobody would have predicted that these two would soon become intimately involved and come up with a very sinister murder plan.

An affair with Gray

Judd Gray was two years older than Ruth but the age difference was insignificant when compared to the one with her husband. He was a quiet, skinny man who didn't attract too much attention. Dedicated to the art of making corsets, Judd had plenty of experience by being an apprentice to some of New York's finest corset designers, which led to his business success. He was also married to his high school sweetheart with one child in tow.

While his wife considered their marriage to be stable, Judd always wanted more. He longed for a connection he had with his own mother and couldn't find the same affection in his wife. And this is what he saw in Ruth when he met her in 1925. She was strong and domineering which attracted him right away. They became lovers pretty quickly and would often talk about their deepest desires. Ruth trusted him and had no reservations discussing her loveless marriage with Albert.

They made the Waldorf Astoria Hotel their secret love nest and were regulars there so the staff didn't ask too many questions. After making love, Judd and Ruth would go down to the bar and drink until early hours. This is when their talks would take a different direction. Ruth started mentioning getting rid of her husband because she simply didn't love him anymore and would leave subtle hints that Albert was abusing her in order to make Judd furious. He wasn't interested in aiding her in a murder back then and would just brush these remarks off.

Since the affair was getting pretty serious, Ruth didn't have any reservations in front of her lover. She didn't hesitate to bring up the hatred she felt towards her husband, who she often referred to as the 'old crab'. She would later reveal that she had tried to kill her husband several times, her methods failing because she wanted to always make it look like an accident.

The first attempt was with gas in the middle of the night while her husband was asleep. Ruth exited the house with her daughter and waited until her husband was asphyxiated. But sensing that something was not right, Albert woke up. He didn't think twice about it and thought that the gas leakage was a simple malfunction.

Albert loved to work on his car so Ruth tried to use this against him. She closed the garage door while he was still inside with the car engine running. Ruth hoped that he would suffocate from the exhaust fumes. However, her husband exited the garage before it was too late. He still had no idea that his wife was behind this murder attempt.

Just like the majority of woman killers back in the day, Ruth tried to poison her husband as well. Albert loved to drink alcohol when he was relaxing in his study so she added a couple of drops of mercury into his whiskey glasses. Albert would get sick briefly but he still managed to pull through. Ruth was clearly frustrated with her solo attempts because they were not going anywhere so it was time to get some help. She trusted Judd and their affair has been going strong for more than two years. She told him that killing her husband was the only way she could get the insurance money but she couldn't do it alone. The two then started to plan the murder.

The killing of Albert Snyder

After Ruth signed Albert up for a $48,000 life insurance policy, she and her lover agreed that the crime should take place on 19th of March 1927 because the entire Snyder family would be out of the house that day.

Ruth's lover Judd would travel from his home in Syracuse to Queens Village, a nervous wreck. He drank hard liquor throughout the trip in order to try and calm his nerves. A quiet man, he didn't have the courage to complete his lover's plan without some kind of alcoholic aid. Since the Snyders were at a party and would not be back for quite some time, Judd entered their home and hid in an unused spare bedroom. Ruth had prepared a makeshift murder tool kit which included chloroform, a dumbbell, and a pair of rubber gloves.

Ruth, Albert, and their daughter Lorraine returned home long after midnight and Albert went straight to bed. Judd was still in the spare bedroom so Ruth used this opportunity to sneak in and make love to him with the sleeping Albert just a couple of feet away. It would prove to be their best sexual thrill yet. After completion, they rested for a few minutes before Ruth led Judd into the master bedroom where Albert was asleep.

Since Ruth left a dumbbell on a window in the spare bedroom, they decided to use it as a primary murder weapon. With both lovers standing on the opposite sides of the bed, Judd raised it and hit unsuspecting Albert in his head. Albert was almost fully covered with a blanket so Judd couldn't see exactly where he was hitting.

But Judd was physically weak. He only grazed Albert with the dumbbell, waking him up. Startled, Albert rose out of the bed and came after his attacker. The lover started panicking and screaming but Ruth swiftly moved to the other side, grabbed the dumbbell from Judd's hands and finished the business. She smashed the weapon down on her husband's head, knocking him unconscious. She then proceeded to strangle him with a wire.

The deed done, they listened quietly for a few moments, fearing that young Lorraine would wake up.

She didn't.

The lovers then sat down in the kitchen and discussed how they should proceed. With Albert dead, the next step was to stage a robbery. They returned to the bedroom to set up the crime scene by tying up both of Albert's hands and feet. Ruth laid out a pistol, bullets and the chloroform. She left the wire around Albert's neck. Once they were done with the corpse, Judd tied Ruth up and gagged her mouth. They took a couple of expensive jewelry pieces which were laying around the house and hid them.

Judd exited the house then Ruth ran to her daughter's room and banged on the door. The little girl was terrified to see her mother bounded and she removed the gag from her mouth. Ruth told her they have been robbed and that she needs to get to their neighbors and call the authorities. Lorraine did so and the police quickly arrived at the scene of the crime. They discovered Albert's body in their shared bedroom and the scene looked terrifying. Ruth told them that she and Albert were asleep when the robbers entered the house, hit her husband in the head, strangled him with a wire, tied her up, and took valuables from them such as jewelry and money. She listed everything that was apparently removed from the house. She couldn't describe the intruders but was sure that they were of Italian descent. After a brief inspection of the house, the police found her jewelry hidden underneath a mattress which raised a lot of questions. Ruth immediately became the number one suspect for the murder of Albert Snyder.

When the investigators told her that they located the items in the house, Ruth became a bit nervous but quickly composed herself. One detective glanced at Ruth's address book and saw Judd Gray's name in it. He asked her who he was and Ruth replied with: "Did he confess?" This detail revealed so much to the police. They started interrogating Ruth because it was obvious that she knew much more than initially thought. She told everything to the police but blamed her "jealous" lover who wanted to get her husband out of the picture. Once they got the name of Ruth's paramour, the investigators drove to Syracuse where Judd Gray was staying at the time. As soon as he opened the hotel room door, he knew what was going on and started wailing.

Judd Gray didn't even try to pretend that he had nothing to do with the murder. As a matter of fact, he started talking immediately, telling the investigators about Albert's life insurance and all the money

Ruth would get once he was dead. He included every single detail of the murder as well as how they staged the scene. But Judd placed the blame on his lover, saying that she made him do it and that he couldn't protest it. It was clear that these lovebirds were turning against each other and only looking after themselves in the process. So the media and the public were about to witness one interesting trial filled with bitterness and quarrels between Judd Gray and Ruth Snyder because neither of them wanted to take the fall for the murder.

The trial of Ruth Snyder and Judd Gray

The trial was scheduled to begin in April of 1927 at the Queens County Courthouse. The case was heavily covered by the media and the accused were nicknamed the Granite Woman and the Putty Man due to their physical appearance and the way they carried themselves. Hundreds of people waited in front of the courthouse in order to get in and listen to the proceedings. They treated the trial as an entertainment and wanted to hear every single detail. The tickets were sold out in an instant but that didn't stop citizens to stand in front of the building. Vendors set up tiny stands, selling macabre souvenirs that represented the case, such as small dumbbells.

Ruth blamed Judd for the murder, while Judd told everyone that she made him do it. Since he was shorter and seemed weaker than Ruth, the public believed in his version of the story. Ruth Snyder was presented as a ruthless woman who would do anything to get rid of her husband and collect his insurance money. On the other hand, Judd was seen as a man who was deeply in love with this cold and calculating woman. But the prosecution wasn't buying this and they put them both on trial together as conspirators.

The prosecution was led by an experienced and accomplished lawyer Richard Newcombe. Edgar Hazelton and Dana Wallace were Ruth's defense and they claimed that Judd was behind the murder and trying to put the blame on a widow. Of course, Judd's defense team presented him as a weak man who would do anything for the woman he loved. With a total of three narratives presented in the courtroom, it was hard to determine the outcome right away.

Both of them were facing a death penalty so the stakes were very high. Ruth's lawyers tried to convince the judge of her innocence by saying that a mother and a devoted wife could never harm her husband and that her lover made the plan on his own. Judd's team changed up the narrative a bit by saying that before he met Ruth, Judd led a quiet and normal life. But once she entered the picture, Judd's behavior changed and he was controlled by her. They presented her as a dangerous seductress who always got what she wanted from men. After all, she had numerous other affairs before she "caught Judd in her web".

Their tactics were working with the general population because Judd became the more trustworthy of the two. The media outlets continued to cover the trial and Judd was getting all the sympathy while Ruth was despised. But the judge wouldn't be swayed by the journalists and the spectators who were on Judd's side. The trial ended after one month with a shocking verdict – both Ruth Snyder and Judd Gray were found guilty for the murder of Albert Snyder. They were sentenced to death by execution.

Post-trial and execution

As soon as they heard the verdict, Ruth Snyder and Judd Gray were transported to Sing Sing Death House. Sing Sing was a famous prison in the state of New York and it held some of the most notorious criminals of the time. Ruth was the sole woman in the Death House during her stay and she avoided socializing with the rest of the inmates. She closed up completely and started writing books and letters obsessively. She managed to get her story published in the New York Daily Mirror and it was called My Own True Story—So Help Me God! Her writing was erratic and the storyline seemed completely disorganized which told a lot about her state of the mind after the imprisonment.

Ruth claimed that her lifestyle was to blame for the crime and that she should have remained faithful to her husband Albert. She spent a good portion of her story warning other girls not to seek lovers or have any extramarital relationships that could endanger them. Ruth clearly states: "I wish a lot of women who may be sinning, could come here and see what I have done for myself through sinning and maybe they would do some of the thinking I have done for months and they would be satisfied with their homes and would stop wishing for things they should try to get along without when they can't have them." Her writing became more troubling after a couple of months of incarceration. It appeared that she had completely lost her mind prior to the execution, focusing her anger on Judd.

It is also important to mention that Ruth had many fans and would receive numerous letters every week. Men who liked dominant women were enchanted by her height and stature, as well as the fact that she was presented as cold hearted in the media. She had over 150 proposals from different suitors who were hoping that the Governor might release her from Sing Sing and that they could live happily ever after.

The hard times were only beginning for Judd once he entered Sing Sing. The sympathy he gathered from the public for being weak completely backfired in prison. The inmates had no respect for him and would avoid Judd at any cost. After all, he blamed a woman for a crime he was clearly guilty of. A mindset like that was a sign of weakness which was often looked down upon in jail. But this didn't prevent Judd from socializing with the men who were in adjacent cells and they were his only friends.

The execution date was set for January 12th, 1928 and when that day came, Ruth was the first on the electric chair. It was customary to completely shave a prisoner's head before they were placed on the chair but they bent the rules for Ruth. The hair was removed from the top of her head, leaving the rest untouched. She started screaming and tossing around as soon as she entered the room. The last bits of her sanity was gone because she knew what awaited her in just a couple of minutes. The guards had to drag her to the chair because she was in a clear state of shock.

As the black mask was placed over her head and electrodes were set tightly on her skin, Ruth started to pray. The electricity was released by Robert G. Elliott who was the executioner, and Ruth was gone after two minutes. During the execution, a photographer who was in the audience managed to get a snapshot of dying Ruth. The cameras weren't allowed in Sing Sing but he smuggled it in around his ankle. It was custom made and pretty small so it wasn't easily detectable. That photo became well-known because it was published in every newspaper the day after the execution. It was also the first image of someone being executed in Sing Sing that was seen by the public.

Judd walked towards the chair on his own. He was clearly scared but didn't make a scene. He said a prayer with a priest as the sweat ran down his face. The guards struggled to place the leather mask over his face but once they were done, the electricity was released and Judd was dead.

The aftermath

Since this case received heavy media coverage back in the day, it did inspire numerous plays and movies in the years that followed. It was a perfect blueprint for the film noir genre and many Hollywood directors borrowed details from the crime in order to make the story more realistic. The best example is The Postman Always Rings Twice that has clear connections to the murder of Albert Snyder.

The camera which was used to capture Ruth's last moments became a part of Smithsonian's National Museum of American History display due to its unusual design and the cultural role it played. The image Ruth on the electric chair is used in some history school books to this day.

Little is known about the life of Ruth's daughter Lorraine. She was really young when her mother killed her father so the chances are she was either placed in foster care or some relatives took her in. Her whereabouts remained unknown.

SARA ALDRETE AND THE SERIAL KILLERS OF DEVIL'S RANCH

EARLY LIFE

Sara Aldrete was born on September 6, 1964 in Matamoros, Tamaulipas, Mexico. As a teen, Sara was allowed to cross the border and attend Porter High School in Brownsville, Texas while her father supported the family working as an electrician. Teachers were fond of Sara as she was a well-behaved student who excelled academically. Her guidance counselor advised her to attend college immediately after graduation but Sara opted to marry instead. At the age of nineteen, she tied the knot with thirty-year old Miguel Zacharias on Halloween Day in 1983. The union did not last last, however, as they were separated and divorced within five months.

Two years later, Sara gained legal status as an American citizen. She enrolled at Texas Southmost College, a two-year school in Brownsville. She had been admitted on a work study program that minimized some of the tuition costs as she worked as both an aerobics teacher and assistant secretary in the school's athletic department.

Sara started classes in January of 1986 as a physical education major. At 6-feet-1 and with model good looks, she was a striking figure around campus.She became one of thirty-three students selected from over a 6,500 member student body to be included in the school's Who's Who directory for 1988. An active student on the campus, she organized a Booster club for the school's soccer squad as well as playing for the girl's volleyball team.

After the dissolution of her marriage, however, she had to move back home with her parents in Matamoros. They had constructed a patio/stairwell outside her second floor room so she could have some semblance of privacy. Sara came home on weekends and during the school breaks, hoping to transfer to a four-year program wherein she could receive a teaching certificate.

Her height and lithe physique caught the eye of many men, in particular Gilberto Sosa, a drug dealer who had ties with the powerful Hernandez family. She began dating Sosa while nurturing an interest in the religion of *Santería*. She learned about the religion's rituals and history during an anthropology class, immediately becoming obsessed. Ironically, this interest would coincide with meeting the man who would take her on a trip into darkness that she would never escape from.

"She would cross that border to Mexico," Lt George Gavito said. "And she would become somebody else."

GODFATHER AND GODMOTHER

Sara was driving through Matamoros on July 30th, 1987 when she nearly got into a car accident with a young man driving a luxury Mercedes-Benz. The young man got out of the car acting apolegetic. Sara was immediately taken by his good looks and well-spoken nature. His introduced himself as Adolfo Constanzo. They exchanged information and Adolfo expressed excitement when he learned that Sara shared the same birthday as his mother.

What Sara didn't know was that the near miss on the Matamoros street was carefully choreographed. Adolfo had been stalking Sara's boyfriend, Gilberto, assessing how much power he had in the drug dealing Hernandez organization.

Adolfo quickly befriended Sara and seduced her with his knowledge of the occult. In a subsequent meeting, Adolfo met the couple together, completely ignoring Gilberto's offer of a handshake and focusing his attention exclusively on Sara.

Later, an anonymous phone call informed Gilberto that Sara was dating someone else. The drug dealer went into a jealous rage and confronted Sara. She denied the allegations but he broke off the relationship anyway.

Sara then turned to Adolfo for comfort. He told her that he knew that Gilberto would break up with her as he had seen her future in a tarot card reading. Adolfo proceeded to "comfort" Sara by seducing her but their physical relationship would not last.

"Sara started dating Constanzo until she found out he was gay," Gavito said. "She said 'no problem'. But he told her what was he was involved in and she introduced him to the Hernandezes. So it was Sara that was the one that connected all of this people together."

Adolfo wanted a meeting with the leader of the Hernandez family, Elio, and Sara arranged for that to happen. Adolfo saw that he could influence drug dealers with his dark magic and earn a nice living for himself. Charming Elio Hernandez would be step one toward that goal.

When Sara returned to the college, her classmates noted that her demeanor changed significantly. Sara obsessed on witchcraft and magic in every conversation. She wanted to argue on the merits between good and evil.

Sara eventually left her studies behind and Adolfo welcomed her into his growing cult. He christened her as "La Madrina", the Godmother. He himself was "El Padrino", the Godfather.

WHO WAS ADOLFO CONSTANZO?

Adolfo was born in Miami, FL on November 1st, 1962 by a fifteen year old girl who would subsequently have three children by three different men. His mother, named Delia Aurora Gonzalez, had her son blessed by a Haitian priest who practiced *palo mayombe*, a form of witchcraft that owes its origins to the Congo but was passed down to Cuba and Puerto Rico with the settlement of slaves.

The boy's mother was excited when the Haitian priest pronounced that her six month old child was "chosen" and "destined for great power."

Delia moved the family to San Juan, Puerto Rico shortly after his baptism. Adolfo's childhood was steeped in the teachings of the dark imaginings of his mother. She taught him the rituals of her bizarre religion even as he became an altar boy at the local Catholic church.

When Adolfo was ten, his mother moved her growing family back to Miami. They once again met with the Haitian priest and young Adolfo began an apprenticeship under the man.

A MOTHER FROM HELL

Adolfo's mother Delia was arrested over thirty times. Her rap sheet included shoplifting, passing false checks, grand theft and child neglect. Her punishment, however, was always lenient and she was never sentenced to anything more than probation. She attributed her ability to escape jail stints to the spells she cast under *palo mayombe* and she passed down this belief system to her son.

A true tenant from hell, she left every apartment she stayed in a vandalized mess. Delia left the walls and floors bloodstained with the remains of animals that she sacrificed. Living in a section of Miami known as the Coral Park Estates, Delia lorded over her neighbors in a reign of terror. Earning her reputation as a witch, Delia was vindictive with anyone who dared inspire her wraith. Neighbor Elena Menendez found a dead goose on her door step with its head wrapped in a red handkerchief. Carmen Reiganda opened her door to find a decapitated chicken on her porch after her son had gotten into an argument with Delia.

Mother and son left a legacy of fear behind in the small Miami neighborhood and the majority of the people were afraid to talk about them.

"Everyone here is worried (Adolfo)will come back to get them for talking," said one man. "I've completely protected my house, and if they come by, I'll blow them away."

LIKE MOTHER, LIKE SON

Adolfo inherited both his mother's religion and criminal ways. He indulged in Miami's gay bars during his teens and earned a living through petty theft. He found school to be a burden and was only interested in learning about black magic. The boy barely graduated from high school and dropped out of junior college after one half-hearted semester.

He continued to obsess about witchcraft with his Haitian priest mentor. They formed a team to rob graves at midnight to stock the priest's lair with dead bodies. They created voodoo dolls and sprinkled blood over them to curse people that crossed them.

The philosophical tenets of *palo mayombe* laid the foundation for Constanzo's future drug dealing endeavors. The belief system places no value judgments on the individual, there is no "good" or "evil" magic. Criminals familiar with the practice used it to protect them from the law but the Haitian priest had a solemn warning for his young student.

"Let the non-believers kill themselves with drugs," the priest said. "We will profit from their foolishness."

By the age of fourteen, Delia became convinced that her son had psychic abilities. Adolfo claimed to have predicted that President Ronald Reagan would be shot by John Hinckley. Adolfo had a murky vision for his own future, however, as he was arrested twice for shoplifting in 1981, including one incident where he tried to steal a chainsaw.

Two years later in 1983, Adolfo had sworn his allegiance to *Kadiempembe*, the name for Satan in *palo mayombe*. The Haitian priest gave Adolfo his blessing as the boy vowed to worship evil in return for financial gain. The priest initiated Adolfo into the fold with a ritual scarring as he took a knife and sliced arcane symbols into the body of his young student.

"My soul is dead," Adolfo said at the end of the ceremony. "I have no God."

BEGINNING OF A CULT

Blessed with good looks, Adolfo landed a modeling gig in 1983. He traveled to Mexico City for a photo shoot and earned some extra money telling fortunes with tarot cards in the city's dangerous Zona

Rosa (Spanish for "Red Zone", a strip of prostitutes, bars and drug dealings.)

The trip to Mexico netted him his first cult followers which included Martin Quintana Rodriguez, Jorge Montes, and Omar Orea Ochoa. Adolfo had affairs with Quintana and Orea, wherein he would be the "woman" or the "man" in the relationship depending on his mood.

In 1984, Adolfo moved his base of operations to Mexico City permanently. He lived with both Quintana and Orea, engaging in nightly homosexual ménage à trois. He began offering his psychic services around the city, developing a reputation for seeing into the future and offering *limpias*. These were ceremonial "cleansings" for those who thought they were cursed by life or wanted some enemies taken care of.

Adolfo kept records of his dealings with the townfolk and his journals revealed that he had thirty-one regular customers. Some of his patrons would pay up to $4500 for one single ritual. Adolfo gave his customers a menu in which they had a choice of sacrificial animals to choose from. Roosters went for $6, goats $30, boa constrictors $450, zebras $1100, and African lion cubs were $3100.

Adolfo began to target the more successful drug dealers in the area. He would help them schedule shipments and customers based on his own alleged "visions". He would charge exorbitant fees for his "magic" to make dealers and their henchmen invisible to police and remain bulletproof against would-be assassins.

Most of the drug merchants had upbringings that paralleled Adolfo's in that their parents were poor peasants who believed in the supernatural. They made for easy dupes for the charismatic cult leader who had one dealer pay him over $40,000 for his supernatural blessings over a period of three years.

Adolfo always delivered, however, as he realized that at such prices his magic would have to be just that, a magic show spectacle. On one occasion he and three of his followers broke into a Mexico City graveyard and excavated numerous graves for bones. His reputation grew as his stage show became more elaborate. He was soon entertaining physicians, business men, fashion models and a host of transvestite cabaret singers. In a bizarre twist, there were several high-ranking police officials that joined Adolfo's cult. The most notable was Salvador Garcia Alarcon, a lead narcotic investigator and Florentino Ventura Gutierrez who was the head of the Mexican branch of Interpol.

The devotion of these individuals clearly went beyond mere bribery or charm. It soon became apparent that they worshiped the young Satanist as he led them on a tour to all of the pits of hell he could dream up.

A year later, Ventura would introduce Adolfo to the infamous Calzada family, arguably Mexico's biggest drug cartel at the time. Letting his charisma do the work for him, Adolfo won the gang over with an elaborate ritual and they repaid him for his blessings of "magic". By 1987, Adolfo had amassed enough cash for a luxury condo and a slew of high-end cars which included an $80,000 Mercedes-Benz.

"Constanzo made these people believers," Gavito said. "I think it could happen to anybody. Most of these kids came from good families. And they're already involved in moving narcotics. So I think it was easy to graduate into the cult part of it. Because they saw the wealth and they saw the power that Constanzo had."

Adolfo liked to push the envelope, however. Not satisfied with his payments from the drug dealers, he disguised himself as a DEA agent and relieved a Guadalajara dealer of his cocaine stash. He sold the coke through his police connections for a $100,000 profit.

As the stakes rose, so did Adolfo's need to have more over-the-top rituals. It was during this time that he began incorporating human sacrifice into his ceremonies. His callousness in both torturing strangers and his closest friends scared both the dealers and police officials into remaining on his good side if they could.

The Calzada drug cartel bought into Adolfo's act hook, line and sinker. The simple minded drug dealers attributed their continued prosperity and survival to his magical powers. Adolfo sensed his influence over the family and realized that he had became a necessary "good luck" charm to them. In the spring of 1987, Adolfo called for a meeting with the heads of the Calzada family. He demanded to become a full partner in their drug dealing enterprise.

The Calzada family rejected the notion immediately.

Adolfo, however, realized that if he was not going to be given power then he would take it.

On April 30th, 1987 Guillermo Calzada Sanchez and six members of his family disappeared under suspicious circumstances. They were reported missing on May 1st with the authorities discovering remnants of what looked like a Santería ceremony at Calzada's office as they found as melted candles and bones scattered about. A week later, mutilated remains washed ashore on the Zumpango River. The police trolled the river and recovered the seven bodies. All of the corpses showed signs of severe torture: fingers, toes and ears were removed, genitals slashed, a spinal column was excised from one body, two others had their skulls opened with their brains missing.

The body parts of the Calzada drug cartel were now part of Adolfo's growing *nganga* or cauldron, a large iron kettle where he stirred up his "witch brew."

His primary drug competitors now eliminated, Adolfo believed that he was growing stronger in his dark magic and began setting his sights on bigger targets.

The Hernandez family became next on his to do list. Adolfo set up a meeting with the powerful Elio Hernandez through Sara who had been dating his son. Adolfo had received word that the Hernandez cartel had dissension in the ranks and were becoming more vulnerable to competing drug families.

During their talk, Adolfo convinced Elio of the efficacy of the *palo mayombe*. He seduced him with the idea of taking his enemies and sacrificing them to his Satan God. In return, Adolfo promised that his family and drug enterprise would be blessed by the dark forces, that they would become invisible to police and bulletproof.

"Give me fifty percent of the profits," Adolfo said. "And I'll control things."

THE BELIEVERS

In 1987, Adolfo became obsessed with a film called the *The Believers* which starred Martin Sheen and Jimmy Smits. It was a movie that showcased the Santeria and voodoo possession and Adoflo saw himself in the characters. He sought to replicate what he saw on the screen into his own rituals.

"It is not at all surprising that Constanzo and Sara Aldrete were infatuated with the movie *The Believers*," said occult researcher Carl Raschke. "The magical practitioners in the film are portrayed as insuperable and almost all knowing."

Adolfo saw the film as validation for what he was doing, specifically conjuring up the spirit realm to aid him in his crimes. Sara, on the other hand, used the movie as a recruiting tool for prospective members.

"[There is]...a story making the rounds that tells of the night Aldrete persuaded three male friends to screen a video of *The Believers*," Rolling Stone magazine reported. "After the film, say the students, Aldrete stood up and began to preach in strange tones about the occult. 'They had been drinking and they just thought she was trying to be spooky,' said one of the students who knew the boys. 'but they look back on it now and think she must have been serious.'"

THEY MUST DIE SCREAMING

Adolfo's thirst for more power and wealth required that his rituals become more specific and gruesome. He moved his cult to a place called Rancho Santa Elena which was about twenty miles away from Sara's hometown of Matamoros.

On May 28th, 1988, Adolfo murdered a drug dealer named Hector de la Fuente and a farmer named Moises Castillo in sacrifices to his demon God. Not satisfied with the level of sadism he achieved in those killings, he then tortured and mutilated a transvestite named Raul Paz Esquivel. Paz was a former lover of one of Adolfo's original followers, Jorge Montes. The level of torture was extreme as they dismembered Paz's body, turning him into a bloodied pretzel. Paz' dismembered body was then left on a city street only to be discovered by school children.

Sadism and torture became foremost on Adolfo's mind as he sought new ways to increase his depravity. Invariably, he would sodomize his victims before their death, giving them one last indignity. Blood and guts fed his cauldron where Adolfo turned the "stew" like a modern day witch. He believed that the devil he worshiped would be more pleased if his sacrificial victims suffered as much as possible.

"They must die screaming," Adolfo intoned to his followers.

THINKING BIG

On August 10th, 1988, rival drug dealers kidnapped Ovidio Hernandez and his two year old boy. They wanted revenge for being ripped off on an $800k deal.

Adolfo, feeling the need to show off the efficacy of his *palo mayembe*, kidnapped a random stranger off the street and brought him to the ranch. They tortured the man, offering him as a sacrifice to their Satanic God while praying for the safe release of the Hernandez family member and his son.

Three days later, the dealers released Hernandez and the boy without any ransom money being exchanged. The Hernandez family gave full credit to Adolfo and his use of witchcraft.

He had them under his spell...

NO SAMPLES FOR YOU

Three months later, a 35-year old ex-policeman turned cult member named Jorge Valente de Fierro Gomez was caught using drugs, stealing from Adolfo's stash.

Adolfo decided to make an example out of his follower as he didn't want any of his members to partake in the drugs. The ex-cop became yet another sacrificial offering to *Kadiempembe*.

On Valentine's Day of 1989, Adolfo's group captured three competing drug dealers and tortured them to death. They dismembered the bodies and added them to the gruesome brew. A week later, another sacrificial victim had been kidnapped but the man put up such a lengthy fight that the group was forced to kill him before he could be tortured. The followers continued their quest to acquire victims. They came upon a 14-year old boy and killed him before realizing that the teen was a cousin of Elio Hernandez.

The boy cried uncontrollably as Adolfo's henchmen had the knife to his throat. Adolfo decided that the boy could be added to the brew because he was too sad. If they sacrificed the boy, then the demon god would be sad. So they killed the boy and went out to the streets to find another young boy.

Adolfo did this because he wanted to acquire the boy's youth. When he wanted "youth" he would have a young boy kidnapped and sacrificed. When he wanted "strength", he would have a strong man kidnapped and dismembered into his brew.

SPECIAL BLESSING NEEDED

By this time, Adolfo had amassed over 800 kg of marijuana that his followers had stolen from another gang. He thought he needed a special blessing to ship the large amount across the Rio Grande. His followers kidnapped another stranger off the streets but Adolfo was not satisfied with the level of sadism they had achieved in torturing the man. He felt that his demon overlord, *Kadiempembe*, would require a new benchmark in torture and pain.

"Bring me someone I can use," Adolfo said. "Someone who will scream."

He also wanted someone smart, someone who had medical training. He instructed his followers to keep their ears out and find an American college student who was going into the medical field.

The next morning, his followers brought in a young college student named Mark Kilroy.

SPRING BREAK HORROR

Matamoros had been a popular hangout for college students on spring break for decades. Students would come upon the small Mexican city looking to let loose in the uninhibited foreign soil that offered prostitution, nudie bars, booze and drugs.

By March of 1989, however, the town had over sixty unsolved disappearances over the course of three months. Unfortunately, this did not deter the usual contingent of American collegians from descending upon the town and enjoying the nightlife.

Mark Kilroy was one of those tourists.

A popular high school student, he played on the basketball and golf teams. He served on the student council and graduated 14th in a class of 210. He initially enrolled at Tarleton State on a basketball scholarship but transferred to the University of Texas after two years, giving up his basketball aspirations to concentrate on his pre-med courses. He was, by all accounts, an upstanding young man.

His father, Jim Kilroy, recalled that when his son was in high school, he would sometimes go to Mark's bedroom to make sure he was studying. He would find the young man reading his Bible instead. "What do you do?" Kilroy asked as he recalled the memory of his son. "He needs to study. But do you go in and tell your son to quit reading the Bible?"

Mark had trekked to Mexico for the spring break with three friends who were all his former classmates at Santa Fe High in Texas.

"The whole semester," a friend recalled. "That (the trip) was all we talked about."

They spent the night enjoying the Mexican food and drinking. They chatted with some girls visiting there from Kansas then returned without incident to their rooms at the Sheraton Hotel on South Padre Island over 20 miles away.

The second night would be quite different. They spent the evening drinking and then around 2 o'clock in the morning they began walking toward the bridge which connected Matamoros with the Texas border town where they had parked their car. Two of Mark's friends walked ahead while Mark and Bill Huddleston lingered about twenty feet behind. Huddleston briefly stepped into an alley to urinate. Mark waited on the street.

When Huddleston came back onto the street he could not find Mark anywhere. There were no signs or sounds of struggle.

THE ABDUCTION

Four of Adolfo's followers had kidnapped Mark. They had been driving a red pick up truck along the main drag of Matamoros, tailing the group unnoticed.

When they spotted Mark alone, they offered him a ride.

"They all had badges that said 'state police,'" Gavito said referring to the fact that Adolfo's followers disguised themselves as cops. "They all had jackets that said police on them. They had red lights in their car. They ran around Matamoros like they were police officers. When (Mark) went off to use the bathroom that was the perfect time. They went up to him, they badged him, they put him in a car, they told him he was under arrest for being drunk. They drive down about two blocks. They pull over, they all get out, the policemen, the guys 'acting' as policemen. They wait for the other car to show up. (Mark) jumps out and starts running."

Mark Kilroy ran for two blocks. The Constanzo crew chased him down yelling "freeze".

"(Mark) being the well educated boy that he is," Gavito said. "Who was brought up to respect the law, when he heard the word 'freeze', he stopped. He was half a block from getting back on the main drag where there was two thousand kids partying. And he stopped, they handcuffed him, they threw him back in the car, they took him back to the ranch. They tied him up and they put him in the back of the Suburban."

He was given food and told he would not be harmed.

Twelve hours later, however, he would be sacrificed.

Kilroy was the only American kidnapped by the cultists. He also came from an affluent family including an uncle that worked for the U.S. Customs Service. His father was a chemical engineer and his mother a volunteer paramedic. The family were devout Catholics, active in their local church.

The response from from the public was immediate. There was a $15,000 reward for information leading to his return or the arrest of his kidnappers.

Yellow bows graced the churches of his hometown and beyond. Dozens of people joined the search for Kilroy, with hundreds of flyers being handed out around the town. San Antonio Mayor Henry Cisneros lobbied Mexican authorities to find the young man.

"I had worked with the Mexican police for over twenty years," Lt. George Gravito recalled. "Best cooperation you've ever had in your life. All of a sudden, I ran into a wall. No cooperation. The state police was telling us that (Mark) was involved in narcotics. But they wouldn't tell me where they're getting the information. This guy was corrupt. What we're meeting with right here on the border, one day you're investigating a crime in Brownsville, Texas and tomorrow morning you're investigating it in Matamoros, Mexico. It's not your jurisdiction and you have to know how to move around. You can't step on the wrong toes because they're gonna kick you out of the country."

The Matamoros police interrogated over one hundred known criminals in the area in the search for Kilroy. They beat their legs with clubs and sprayed soda water mixed with hot sauce into their nostrils.

They came up with nothing.

ONE MORE SACRIFICE

Adolfo had used the sacrifice of Kilroy in his mind to ensure the safe shipment of his marijuana. But now, he thought he needed yet another special sacrifice to his palo mayombe overlord.

Adolfo decided to target Sara's former boyfriend, Gilberto Sosa.

On March 28th, 1989, Sosa became the cult's final sacrifice as the marijuana made its way across the Rio Grande on April 8th.

Adolfo's alleged psychic abilities would fail him, however, as his depraved empire would soon come to an end in a way that he didn't foresee...

PURE LUCK

The police drew no leads for two weeks until they came across a "happy accident" on April 10th of that year...

"We were lucky," Gravito recalled. "What helped us in this investigation was, we had been working on some narcotic cases. DEA Brownsville had been working real close with *un commandante* in Matamoros. That *commandante* was Juan Benitez Ayala. He was the head of the federal police assigned to the Matamoros area. This man, Juan Benitez Ayala, I'll say was about five feet tall. But he probably stood about eight foot tall. I mean when this guy walked in anywhere people were scared of him. He worked and that's all he did.

"You didn't see him in bars. You didn't see him in restaurants. And the reason he didn't go to bars or restaurants, one, he was afraid someone might put something in his drink and kill him. The guy was taking down some powerful people in Mexico and we went to talk to him."

"I told him we got this problem with this state police guy, he says these kids were involved in narcotics, and I assure you that they weren't. We had helped them on some cases, we had busted some big people (because) we had shared some information. So he put his people to work. And every time we had a lead, we'd call him, we'd go over there, we'd kick doors down, you know, you don't need a search warrant, the search warrant IS the federal police and nobody gets in your way."

The Mexican police had erected roadblocks and began a random drug roust in areas of Matamoros unrelated to the Kilroy disappearance. They had a policy of targeting only the low level runners and leave the heads of the drug operations alone.

Serafin Hernandez was the epitome of the low-level drug dealer. He was the twenty year old nephew of Elio Hernandez and a well known trafficker. During this drug roust, Serafin came across the police checkpoint and was followed. He unknowingly led the officers to the innocuous looking cattle ranch. A shabby looking corral marked the front with a tar paper and wood shack that stood in the rear of the winding, unmarked road.

It was Rancho Santa Elena, the home of Constanzo's cult.

The police waited a week and returned en masse, arresting both Serafin and another dealer named David Serna Valdez. The interrogations began and the two dealers proved to be cocky witnesses. They claimed they were "protected" by supernatural powers, of course referring to the spells that Adolfo had cast.

Inside, the police found a horror chamber beyond the imagination of any snuff film. The 15x25 foot shed was saturated with blood and smelled of rotting flesh. They found human brains, hair, teeth and skulls. Some spines had been crafted into necklaces. Scattered around were machetes and white votive candles in a box that bore a picture of *Our Lady of Guadalupe.*

The press nicknamed Rancho Santa Elena as the "Devil's Ranch."

"I thought in my twenty two years of law enforcement I had seen everything," a Texas deputy said. "I hadn't. As we drew near, you could smell the stench…blood and decomposing organs. In a big, cast iron pot there were pieces of human bodies and a goat's head with horns."

MAKING THE CONNECTION

"About two o'clock in the morning I get a call from *el commandante*," Gavito recalled. "We found (Mark) he said. 'You found (Mark)? You kidding?' he said no. We found (Mark). Where? He said he's buried in a ranch outside of Matamoros. I asked him how? Or who? He said there was a caretaker that also lived near the ranch. When he arrested Serafin, he picked him up too, the caretaker, but he didn't file charges against him. But he kept him under house arrest and the caretaker saw a picture of (Mark) on top of the table. And he pointed to it and said 'I know that boy'. 'How do you know him?' 'I was feeding him. I was giving him bread. I untied one of his arms so he could sit up and eat' because they had him tied to the back of a Suburban."

El Commandante then began interrogating Serafin. Without prompting, Serafin began offering information on how he knew Mark Kilroy, admitting that he was the one who kidnapped him.

"This guy was volunteering all of this information," Gavito said. "I mean usually in Mexico you have to go, you know, I guess its something you have to know when you get arrested, that they're going to torture you to get the truth out of you. But I've never heard of anybody just confessing this easily as Serafin. And we kinda talked a little bit and the name Constanzo had come up on his investigations. Serafin had said that they had kidnapped (Mark) because the *Padrino*, Constanzo, wanted somebody who was studying medicine because they were doing some kind of witchcraft."

"They were going to use Mark's brain to give it to this pot that they had. And I didn't understand what he was talking about and I said did you have to torture this guy and he said 'no, this guy (Serafin) thinks that bullets do him no harm and the police can't hurt him he thinks that this guy, this Constanzo is gonna come in here and take him out of here."

"It's our religion," Serafin said. "Our voodoo."

George Gavito recalled that during Serafin's confession he repeatedly made reference to the aforementioned film, *The Believers.*

"I remember I didn't understand what he was telling me," Gravito said. "I said, 'Is it Santeria?' And he said, 'Yeah, yeah, Santeria, voodoo, man.' And then he kept on saying, 'The Believers, The Believers, The Believers.'"

"Elio made [Serafin] Garcia a priest, but Garcia didn't really know what he was practicing because all he had on his mind was the movie."

Serafin told the authorities about El Padrino, the Godfather, as being Adolfo Constanzo. He revealed the details of Adolfo's ritual of African magic, palo mayombe. "Adolfo ordered the slayings," Serafin said. He revealed that the Godfather had tortured and sodomized his victims before killing them. They would then mutilate the bodies and harvest the organs for his witches brew.

SCENE OF THE CRIME

Serafin was brought back to the Devil's Ranch with Ayala and Gavito, both police officials not expecting the level of depravity they were about to investigate.

"We asked him where the body was," Gavito recalled. "And he said 'which body?' Just like that. 'Which body?' 'Man,' El Commandante says. 'Man, if you're playing games with me' and he got pissed off. And he (Serafin) says 'hold on, which body you want?'"

"'What do you mean, which body!'" El Commandante screamed.

"There's a bunch of bodies out here," Serafin said. "Which one do you want?"

"What do you mean?"

"Yeah," Serafin began walking through the corrals. "There's one buried here, there's one buried there."

"How many?"

"I don't know."

"Where's Mark?"

"Over there in the corner."

"Where?"

"I don't remember exactly," Serafin said as he started walking to a corner of the corral. "But I think it is where that wire is."

The police looked down and saw a coat hanger half-buried in the dirt.

"Why a coat hanger?"

"Oh, because Constanzo wanted to make a necklace," Serafin said. "With Mark's backbone. So after we killed them and everything we ran wire through his back, through the spinal cord, so that later on we could just come and get it out and he could make a necklace."

Disgusted and angry, Benitez-Ayala handed Serafin a shovel, forcing him to dig up the body of Mark.

During the dig, Serafain revealed that Constanzo had killed Mark with one machete slice to the back of his head. He began revealing more details of other killings, matter of factly and without feeling. At one point he even asked if the police we're going to order food because he was getting hungry.

El Commandante Benitez-Ayala became enraged. He took out his Uzi and fired the weapon into the air out of frustration.

"You don't think bullets can hurt you?" he asked Serafin.

"No," Serafin replied.

El Commandante then began emptying his entire clip.

"That's when the kid's eyes opened up," Gavito recalled, remembering how frightened Serafin became. "I mean his eyes opened up when he heard that sound, I mean it freaked us all out because we didn't realize what was going on. He (Serafin) went from being a believer to being a disbeliever pretty quick. He went back to being a normal person."

Serafin suddenly snapped out of his brainwashed state.

"I don't know why they got us to do this," Serafin said.

"All of a sudden it was 'why' they got us to do this," Gavito said. "It just changed."

His body unearthed, Kilroy's skull had been split open and his brain removed. The police then found a nearby shed wherein they located Adolfo's *nganga*, a cast-iron cauldron that was stained with blood, body parts and numerous sticks, the "palos" of *palo mayombe*.

Inside the kettle were spiders, scorpions and the brain of Kilroy. His brain had been boiled in blood over an open fire along with a turtle shell, a horseshoe, a spinal column and other human bones.

FAILING MAGICAL POWERS

Adolfo was surprised at the reaction to Kilroy's disappearance. He was used to his killings not gaining any notoriety at all. Even after the fact, three of the unearthed victims have never been identified and only a handful were reported missing.

The next day, all hell break loose for the cult members. Four members of the Hernandez family were arrested and the cash from their big marijuana sale was confiscated. The police began unearthing bodies from the ranch on April 11th, finding more bodies in a nearby orchard.

Feeling the heat, Adolfo went on the run with Sara, and his two lovers Martin and Omar. A Hernandez family hit man named Alvaro De Leon Valdez, nicknamed "El Duby", came along as well.

Adolfo's first instinct was to go to Miami where he could be with his mother. He decided to stay travel to Mexico City, however, using the homes of followers and friends of followers to hide.

The gruesome discoveries made the rounds in tabloid television. Geraldo Rivera produced a segment on the murders. There were false sightings of the cult being reported in the United States. Adolfo was claimed to have been seen in Chicago where people mistakenly labeled him as part of the Windy City Mafia. Sara was reportedly seen skulking around schools throughout various border towns, threatening to kidnap and kill ten white kids for every one of her followers that were jailed in Mexico. There was a church located in Pharr, Texas that was burned down after rumors that some if its members were connected to Adolfo's cult. Serafin Sr, a drug dealer and follower of Adolfo, was found and arrested.

The national news did little to shed light on the whereabouts of Adolfo, however. They successfully hid from sight as if their Devil God had swallowed them up and welcomed them into hell...

BETRAYAL IN THE CARDS

Adolfo did a tarot card reading on April 18th, 1989 and supposedly foresaw a betrayal among his followers. He knew that any of the many low level drug runners could have ratted out Serafin Sr and he now looked at his followers with a suspicious eye. He kept a gun close by and did his best to avoid sleep. His paranoia led to angry outbursts against his acolytes.

"They cannot kill you," he warned. "But I can."

The Commandante, Juan Ayala, meanwhile, took the threat of Constanzo's *brujeria* (witchcraft) very seriously.

"He flew in his own brujo (male witch), to take care of him and to take care of all his agents," Gavito said. "To make sure there was not 'bad vibes'. And not only that, but to help him in the investigation. To find out what was the best way to catch Constanzo. He (the witch) told Benitez, 'you wanna catch him? Burn their hut! Burn their nganga! Burn where they were worshiping.'"

"So we got out there one Sunday morning. Took one Mexican television station to cover it because he wanted Constanzo to see this. The brujo puts gasoline around it. They light it up and it starts to burn and we sit there while the whole thing burns to the ground."

Adolfo watched the scene on television as Ayala had hoped. His screen police sifted through what was left at the ranch. He then went into a rage inside the small hideaway apartment, smashing furniture and flipping over the couch for starters.

"He felt raped," Gavito said. "He felt that we had invaded his privacy. That we had done something we shouldn't have. He started losing it."

MOVING ON

Adolfo made one last move with his followers as they found an apartment on Rio Sena in Mexico City.

Sara, finally realizing her life was in danger or needing to now play the role of the victim since the authorities were no doubt closing in, made a handwritten note. She threw it out the bedroom window in the hopes that a Good Samaritan would come along and find it.

The note read:

Please call the judicial police and tell them that in this building are those that they are seeking. Tell them that a woman is being held hostage. I beg for this, because what I want most is to talk—or they're going to kill the girl.

A stranger walking by picked up the note but kept it to himself, thinking it was a joke. Upstairs, however, Adolfo plotted his next getaway move.

"They'll never take me," he said.

MORE RANDOM LUCK

A few days later, police arrived on Rio Sena and began going door to door looking for a missing child. Adolfo saw them from his window and began opening fire with his Uzi not realizing that they were not looking for him.

Over one hundred eighty-police men almost immediately. A fiery battle ensued which lasted almost forty-five minutes. Surprisingly, the only person injured during the crossfire was an officer who was struck by Adolfo's first barrage.

According to Sara, Adolfo ordered his own killing, telling El Duby to shoot him and his right hand man, Martin Quintana Rodriguez.

"He lost it," Gavito said. "He turned on the stove. Put the money on the stove. Started burning money. He started throwing coins out. Just lost it."

"He went crazy, crazy," said El Duby. "He grabbed a bundle of money and threw it and began shooting out the window. He said everything, everything was lost. No one's going to have this money."

"He wanted to die with Martin," Sara said.

Adolfo soon realized he was trapped. He handed his Uzi to El Duby.

"He told me to kill him and Martin," El Duby said. "I told I told him I couldn't do it, but he hit me in the face and threatened that everything would go bad for me in hell. Then he hugged Martin, and I just stood in front of them and shot them with a machine gun."

The police entered the apartment with guns raised but Adolfo and Martin were already dead, their bodies slumped together in a closet. The three remaining cult members, El Duby, Orea, and Sara were captured.

Over twenty rounds were found in autopsied body, possibly indicating that the Mexican police had continued to shoot him port-mortem.

THE TRIALS

El Duby's case was open and shut. He had confessed to the two murders and had no reasonable defense. Sara, however, was a tad different as she initially proclaimed to be a victim but knew too much of the cult's ins and outs to not be considered an accomplice.

After the shootout, fourteen cult members in total were indicted for murder. In August of 1990, El Duby was convicted of the killing of Adolfo and Martin, getting a 35-year prison term. Juan Fragosa and Jorge Montes were convicted to 35 years for the killing of Raul Esquivel.

Omar Orea, one of Adolfo's lovers, died of AIDS before going to trial.

Sara had been acquitted of Adolfo's slaying but was sentenced to a six year term for her criminal associations. She maintained her innocence throughout, stating that she never practiced the *palo malembe* but a "Christian Santeria."

Showing a calm demeanor during her interrogations, Sara expressed sorrow for the murders of Kilroy and the other victims.

American law officials saw Sara as having a split personality. They knew that in private, Sara would lose her "charming aspect" that she revealed when she knew the television cameras were on. She reverted into another self, talking with relish in describing the cult's rituals.

"I would say she has three personalities," a Mexico City attorney general said. "One personality comes out and faces the cameras and denies any involvement in the human slayings, another emerges when she talks to police and the third one comes out when she talks to herself."

American Customs agent Oran Neck spent several days in Mexico City assisting the local police. "Sara has kind of lost touch with reality," Neck said after he questioned her. "Her dual personality is coming up pretty strong right now. When you talk to her without the TV cameras there, she's pretty truthful."

"She gives a lot of data with great detail to investigators. It seems like when the cameras come on, she kind of reverts back to this nice, young, clean-cut kid from Texas Southmost College."

"When the cameras were there, she was real nice," Lt. George Gravito said. "When she was with us, she was the same ol' witch."

SARA'S SENTENCE

"If I had known it (the cult) was like this," Sara said. "I wouldn't have been in it."

Six years after her criminal association sentence was up, Sara was tried again and convicted of several of the murders at the cult's headquarters. She is now serving 30 years in prison.

During an interview with SFGate, Sara claimed that she was tortured by Mexican police after her capture. She said she was stripped, blindfolded, hung upside down, beaten, had her toenails pulled out and was burned inside her vagina in and out. She claims the burns were so severe that a doctor told her she'd never have children.

She also remembers the police shoving her hands into Adolfo's autopsied body at the morgue.

They yelled at her to pull out his heart.

"There is your devil," they mocked. "There is your prince. Kiss him. Kiss him."

The Mexican authorities have denied these claims.

"The witch deserves everything she got," Lt. George Gavito said.

Mark Kilroy's parents have said they have forgiven her but do not want her released. "You have to control a mass murderer," said Jim Kilroy. "What are you going to do? Let her loose and have her murder other people?"

Even after the convictions, some murders from the time period have remained unsolved. Between 1987 and 1989, there were 74 unsolved ritual murders in Mexico City. 14 of these involved children. Adolfo's cult is connected to 16 but there has been no evidence to connect them to the rest.

"We would like to say, yes, Constanzo did them all," prosecutor Guillermo Ibarra said. "And poof, all those cases are solved. And the fact is, we believe he was responsible for some of them, though we'll never prove it now. But he didn't commit all of those murders. Which means someone else did. Someone who is still out there."

SERIAL KILLER JUANA BARRAZA

MARCUS MOORE

Juana Barraza is perhaps the most famous serial killer in all of Mexico's history. Authorities have attributed the death of up to 48 elderly women in Mexico to Juana, and she was found guilty in 2008 of several murders and was sentenced to a total of 759 years in jail for her crimes. Referred to as Mataviejitas, or Little Old Lady Killer, Juana's killing spree and the subsequent police investigation, became national news in Mexico in 2007 and 2008, and led to widespread pressure on the police department to solve the series of crimes against the nation's most vulnerable members of society.

Background

Juana Barraza, or Juana Dayanara Barraza Samperio, was born on December 27, 1958 in the small rural town of Epazoyucan, Hidalgo, located north of the nation's capital of Mexico City. Her father, Trinidad Barraza, was a local police officer and her mother, Justa Samperio, was a prostitute. Juana's mother left her father shortly after Juana's birth to begin a relationship with a married man named Refugio Samperio, was was Justa's stepfather during her childhood.

Juana reportedly suffered from a difficult and violent childhood, living with an extreme alcoholic for a mother. She was illiterate as a child and was often physically and emotionally neglected by her mother. She would later claim that her mother sold her to a strange man named Jose Lugo when she was only twelve years old for just three beers; the man sexually assaulted Juana repeatedly and she became pregnant with a boy. Juana would eventually have a total of four children, although her oldest son died in a robbery attempt at 24 years old.

Prior to becoming famous for her role as a serial killer, Juana was a relatively little-known wrestler who participated in the amateur circuits of *lucha libre*, a famous form of Mexican wrestling that involves the use of masks and significant amounts of stage drama. During her career as a wrestler, she performed under the stage name *La Dama del Silencio*, also known as The Silent Lady in Spanish.

While Juana toured the country as a part of the amateur wrestling circuit in the 1980s and 1990s, she turned to stealing and burglary in 1995 after birthing her fourth child. In 1996, she began robbing elderly people with a friend of hers, setting up a pattern of targeting the elderly that would last throughout her entire criminal career. The two burglars would dress in all-white scrubs and pretend to be nurses in order to gain their victim's trust and access to their homes.

Crimes

Juana's profile as a serial killer was that she consistently targeted elderly women, in their late 60s or older. Many of her victims lived alone and had little contact with local relatives or a strong social circle. Juana would typically befriend the victim, then lure them to their home or a quiet place where she would bludgeon them to death with a heavy object or strangle them with an extension cord that she carried on her person, usually robbing the victim once they were dead.

Juana used several different methods to gain her victims' trust. She would often cruise the streets of poorer neighborhoods, looking for elderly woman who were by themselves and struggling with bags of groceries or other household items. She would then offer to help the elderly women up their set of stairs to their apartments, where she would the kill her victim. Juana would also frequently pose as a government official, complete with an ID badge and government application forms. She would claim that she was going door-to-door to help pensioners apply for their benefits in order to gain their trust and access to their home. She frequently used phone cords, extension cables, tights, or a stethoscope to strangle her victims.

It is suspected that Juana's first victim was Maria de la Luz Gonzalez Anaya, who was murdered on November 25, 2002. Juana gained access to her apartment, likely in order to rob the elderly woman, but ended up killing Maria Gonzalez after the woman made disparaging comments about Juana, angering her and leading to her strangling the victim in a fit of rage.

Several years into her career as a serial killer, Juana Barraza began a romantic relationship with Jose Francisco Torres Herrera, a taxi driver known as *El Frijol*, or The Bean. Together, the two continued her killing spree and began by targeting Carmen Camila Gonzalez Miguel, an 82-year old wealthy woman in Mexico City. While the pair did successfully kill Carmen and escape, this murder led to a widespread police response and investigation into the existence of a serial killer in Mexico City. Carmen Gonzalez was the mother of Luis Rafael Moreno Gonzalez, a well-known and powerful criminologist. Her death led to increased police patrols, a public information campaign, and a collaboration with French investigators, who had recently detained *The Monster of Montmartre*, a prominent French serial killer.

Police Investigation

During the early stages of the investigation into a potential serial killer, the chief prosecutor for Mexico City, Bernardo Batiz, publicly said that he thought the killer had "a brilliant mind, quite clever and careful" and that he suspected the killer was adept at gaining the trust of their potential victims prior to killing them. Several officials believed that the killer was posing as a government benefits counselor who established trust by offering to help the victim secure government benefits like health care and welfare.

There was an odd coincidence which confused the police working on the case and led to detectives investigating misleading information that ultimately delayed Juana's capture. Early on, the police noticed that at least three of the women killed by Juana owned a copy of the *Boy in Red Waistcoat*, a famous painting from the 1700s by French painter Jean-Baptiste Greuze. For some time, police were convinced that the presence of this painting had some important bearing on the case and why the victims were chosen; but, ultimately it became clear that the presence of the painting was mere coincidence and that the police department's focus on this "evidence" was misplaced.

Police were able to determine through their investigation and subsequent in-person interviews that Juana was clinically classified as a psychopath: she did not feel any pain or remorse for actions, and thus had no moral qualms about her actions and their effects. Psychologists say that Juana associated the elderly women that she preyed on with her mother, believing that her actions were a net good because she was removing evil people from the world. Her lack of empathy, combined with her engaging persona and false identity as a government worker, allowed her to gain these women's trust in a small amount of time.

Despite the rash of killings in Mexico City in late 2005 and early 2006, the local police department consistently dismissed any theories of an emerging serial killer and called out such ideas as "media sensationalism." However, police did begin to take reports of a serial killer seriously in November 2005, when they received several witness statements reporting that the killer wore women's clothing, leading them to suspect that the serial killer was actually a transvestite who posed as a woman to gain access to, and trust from, his victims. On one particular occasion, the killer was seen living a victim's house wearing a red blouse.

Once the police department finally did launch a full investigation of the killings, their first action was to launch a city-wide raid of all of the areas frequented by transvestite prostitutes, since they mistakenly believed at that time that the killer was a transvestite who dressed as a female in order to gain the trust of his female victims. A reporter for La Jornada, a popular newspaper in Mexico City, would call the series of raids "ham-fisted" unproductive.

In addition to detaining and questioning all of the city's known transvestite prostitutes, the police also began visiting the local morgue to check fingerprints. They believed that the killer may have committed suicide and that they need only verify the identity of one of the corpses to close the case. This belief would quickly prove to be incorrect.

Despite initial fumbling by the police department and an investigation predicated based upon incorrect assumptions about the killer, the case would soon break open in a very public way. On January 25th, 2006, a suspect was seen fleeing from the home of the now-deceased Ana Maria de los Reyes Alfaro, an 82-year old women living in the Venustiano Carranza section of Mexico City. Ana Alfaro was strangled to death with a stethoscope by Juana Barraza. Luckily for the police, Alfaro was a landlady and one of her new tenants was arriving at her home as Juana attempted to flee the scene of the crime. The tenant nearly bumped into Juana as she rushed out of the building and was the first to see Reyes Alfaro's body. He immediately called the police and was able to provide the description that led to Juana's capture.

In a surprise to both the police, national media, and public, the suspected killer was actually Juana Barraza, a 48 year old amateur wrestler, and a woman that many people would mistake for a kindly grandmother; here was the famed Mexico City serial killer, and the nation was shocked.

Police investigators were initially drawn to the idea of a transvestite serial killer because of composite sketches and witness statements that described the serial killer as a masculine-looking woman. Given these statements and the fact that the vast majority of serial killers are men, they police department completely ignored the possibility that the killer could actually be a "masculine-looking woman," as opposed to a man dressed as a woman.

Despite this initial confusion, police quickly realized that Juana looked remarkably similar to the police sketches that had been composed from witness statements. The more that police learned about Juana, the more that her role as the serial killer made sense. Police initially thought that the killer had to be a man or male transvestite because of the sheer amount of strength required to strangle someone. They thought that it was impossible for a woman possess that much physical strength; however, Juana was no ordinary woman. She was a professional wrestler reportedly capable of bench pressing 200 lbs for multiple sets of ten, a significant sign of strength in any person.

Furthermore, her use of the stethoscope to kill her last victim was in line with witness statements, which had described a government worker with short, dyed-blonde hair and a mole on their face, carrying a stethoscope, benefit forms, and a government ID card.

Once detained, police were quickly able to connect Juana to at least ten other murders using her fingerprints. Mexico City's chief prosecutor at the time, Bernardo Batiz, would tell the media that "Fingerprints match in 10 murder cases, as well as one attempt." In addition, police investigators found several trophies related to the killings in her home, including cutouts of newspaper articles discussing the killings (despite the fact that she is illiterate). Juana admitted to killing Ana Alfaro, but said that she had initially visited the elderly woman's home in order to secure work during laundry and that she killed the woman out of "anger," and not because of any premeditated reason.

Trial

Juana Barraza began her trial for murder in spring 2008, with prosecutors claiming that she was responsible for up to 40 killings over the previous six years. While Juana admitted to killing Ana Alfaro, claiming that she murdered the elderly woman out of anger because she resembled Juana's abusive mother, she claimed that she was innocent of all of the other charges levied against her.

Despite her claims of innocence, Juana was sentenced to prison for 759 years in March 2008, after being found guilty of 11 separate murder charges and an aggravated burglary charge. Given that federal sentences in Mexico are served concurrently and legally the maximum sentence a person can receive is 60 years, it is likely that Juana will die in prison. However, she will be eligible for parole in 2058, when she is 100 years old.

Suspected Victims
Robbery
1995-2001

Juana is suspected of robbing a large, unknown amount of victims during this time period.

Murder

2002

November 24th: Maria de la Luz Gonzalez Anaya (64 years old)

2003

March 2nd: Guillermina Leon Oropeza (84 years old)

July 25th: Maria Guadalupe Aguilar Cortina (86 years old)

October 9th: Maria Duadalupe de la Vega Morales (87 years old)

October 24th: Maria del Carmen Munoz Cote de Galvan (78 years old)

2004

February 20th: Alicia Gonzalez Castillo (75 years old)

February 25th: Andrea Tecante Carreto (74 years old)

March 20th: Carmen Cardona Rodea (76 years old)

March 26th: Socorro Enedina Martinez Pajares (82 years old)

May 24th: Guadalupe Gonzalez Sanchez (74 years old)

June 25th: Esthela Cantoral Trejo (85 years old)

July 1st: Delfina Gonzalez Castillo (92 years old)

July 3rd: Maria Virginia Xelhuatzi Tizapan (84 years old)

July 19th: Maria de los Angeles Cortes Reynoso (84 years old)

August 31st: Margarita Martell Vazquez (72 years old)

September 29th: Simona Bedolla Ayala (79 years old)

October 24th: Maria Dolores Martinez Benavides (70 years old)

November 9th: Margarita Arredondo Rodriguez (83 years old)

November 17th: Maria Imelda Estrada Perez (76 years old)

2005

January 11th: Julia Vera Duplan (60 years old)

February 10th: Maria Elena Mendoza Vallares (59 years old)

April 13th: Maria Elisa Perez Moreno (76 years old)

April 14th: Arturo Patino Barranco (74 years old)

April 19th: Carolina Robledo (79 years old)

April 20th: Ana Maria Velazquez Diaz (62 years old)

June 17th: Celia Villaliz Morales (78 years old)

June 29th: Maria Guadalupe Nunez Almanza (78 years old)

July 5th: Julia Vargas (64 years old)

July 5th: Mario Cruz Flores (84 years old)

July 20th: Emma Armenta Aguayo (80 years old)

August 9th: Emma Reyes Pena (72 years old)

August 11th: Carmen Sanchez Serrano (76 years old)

August 15th: Dolores Concepcion Silva Calva (91 years old)

September 28th: Maria del Carmen Camila Gonzalez Miguel (82 years old)

September 28th: Guadalupe Oliver Contreras (85 years old)

October 18th: Maria de los Angeles Repper Hernandez (92 years old)

2006

January 25th: Ana Maria de los Reyes Alfaro (84 years old)

Juana' Public Response

Juana has repeatedly denied that she is a serial killer, although she has admitted to at least one murder. During her first appearance in court for her trial, she stated "I only killed one little old lady. Not the others. It isn't right to pin the others on me." When she was later asked about her motive for the sole killing that she took responsibility for, she simply said, "I got angry."

Juana has maintained her innocence throughout her trial, verdict and during her current stay in prison, remarking at her verdict, "May God forgive you and not forget me." She has vowed to appeal all but one of the charges she was found guilty of, claiming that her sole killing was a crime of passion against Ana Alfaro on the day she was caught.

TWISTED SISTERS : THE TRUE STORY OF REGINA AND MARGARET DEFRANCISCO

CHAPTER ONE

Regina and Margaret DeFrancisco are two sisters convicted of first degree murder.

On paper, the two sisters look like two girls you would see at a church social.

In school, both were good but not great students. Margaret was the pretty one. She would get all of the attention from the boys but return little interest.

Margaret was a student at Jones College Prep School, a selective public institution that is considered one of the top high schools in Illinois.

A little on the shy side, Margaret had a quick wit and sense of humor. Sweet-looking and pretty, she had avoided any kind of trouble throughout her young life. Her early photos suggest, however, that her subtle smirk was a couldn't contain the narcissism that was growing within.

"You would look at Margaret and see right through her," one of her neighbors said. "It was black, like was nothing there. She didn't seem like she had depth, like she had compassion."

Regina had a love for animals, particularly ponies. She rode horses and in her words, "never lost a show."

Regina was also the more extroverted of the two, wearing her emotions on her sleeve. She could mouth off and had a chip on her shoulder. She also had a thing for 'bad boys', seeing them as a reflection of herself.

"A lot of girls get turned on by the 'thug life'," forensic psychologist Marnie Clark said. "The DeFrancisco sisters definitely fit that mold. They were not out to play Mrs. Cleaver when they grew up. They were attracted to the gang lifestyle. They thought the drama was exciting."

The girls were raised by a single parent, Nora DeFrancisco. Nora raised the two sisters and their brother Joey in the Pilsen neighborhood of Chicago. Their father, Augie DeFrancisco was a small-time burglar and convicted drug dealer who had no involvement in the girl's childhood years. Their maternal grandfather, Gilbert Smith, was a former Chicago cop who was fired from the force in 1960 after admitting that he was "friendly with certain burglars."

Growing up in Pilsen, however, the girls could not avoid rubbing shoulders with gang members. They became enamored with gang culture, learning who fought against who and what the names of the gangs were. There were the Latin Counts, Kool Gang, Villa Lobos, Bishops, among many other offshoots. The girls knew what streets signified what gang members' territory and memorized their hand signals.

"Chicago is simply rife with gangs," Clark said. "It is inescapable, even to those in the more affluent communities. There is still a choice, however. For whatever reason, the DeFrancisco sisters were drawn to the 'thug life'. To a young person, it looks 'cool'.

They are the classic examples of young women who could not see the big picture and thought the thug life was something worth aspiring to."

The two sisters, with their striking brunette looks, could not help but come into the cross hairs of the local gang members. They began wearing dark lipstick and teasing their hair out. Margaret would get a tattoo on her belly. Regina would have the letter "R" tattooed on her leg as well as a drawing of a heart just above her breast. They would hang out on street corners and in front of the local liquor store, chatting up the neighborhood 'gangstas'.

"The changes in their make-up and dress signified the changes in their personality," Clark said. "They grew bored during their time at prep school. Even ashamed. They did not want to see themselves as nerds and hated that aspect of themselves. Starting in eighth grade, it was time to start rebelling. By the time they reached high-school, the thug life was part of their persona. Dark make-up. Tattoos. Hanging out with gang bangers. Alcohol and drugs. But most important, they wanted all the drama that came with that kind of life. Who is out to get who, who dissed who and who shot who became their modus operandi in life."

Grandfather Gilbert, however, had seen this all before as a Chicago cop. He feared that the girls, particularly Regina, would become ensnared by the street gang culture. He tried to obstruct this from happening and found Regina a job with a local periodontist. He figured if he kept the girl busy with school and work it would keep her away from the idiots on the street.

Regina, however, did not have the emotional maturity to see the light. She showed up late for her first couple of shifts then she was fired.

But she had started dating a man named Johnny Rivera, a known member of Chicago's notorious "Latin Kings" street gang. Rivera had a rap sheet as long as "War and Peace" as well as more aliases than a Russian spy

Regina would learn how to package and deal drugs at the foot of Johnny. She would watch him put the cocaine into plastic bags, measuring it out by the ounce. They would drive around town and Johnny would introduce her to his customers, watching as he conducted the deals. The secret handshakes and secret lingo all became apart of Regina's world.

Officially crossing over from innocent prep school girl to drug dealing girlfriend, Regina lived a double life. She did manage to get a part-time job doing data entry work for a local law firm and had enrolled in the local junior college (Harold Washington).

Margaret was getting into trouble as well. Her grades in high school were slipping as she would sneak out at night to be with friends. She would often come to school looking "disheveled" according to one teacher who thought she looked like a child whose parents were going through a divorce.

And there was trouble on the home front.

Neighbors would report hearing the girls fighting with their mother on a daily basis.. The two girls were out of control with no father figure to put them in line. Nora would berate Regina whenever she would act up in school or get arrested and the girls would yell back.

In private, Nora would refer to her daughters as "the bitches".

Things would come to a head when Regina would get arrested for selling cocaine to an undercover cop. A single mom already strapped for cash as she had to support three children on her own, Nora was livid as she paid Regina's bail.

"How are you going to pay me back?" .

"I don't know!"

"Do you know how much it costs to bail you out of jail!" Nora screamed. "You are going to pay me back. You're going to pay me back every penny!"

CHAPTER TWO

"She needs money," Margaret said, her voice full of concern.

"How much?" Oscar asked.

"One thousand dollars. Can you help us out, baby?"

That was the scene set for the twenty-two year old Oscar Velazquez in June of 2000 as he spoke to the sister of his current teenage crush, Regina DeFrancisco. He spotted Regina around the neighborhood of Pilsen and quickly fell for her dark Irish-Italian good looks. Showing off his brand new Z28 Camaro, he chatted up the girls before he asked Regina out for tacos. The two began going out but Regina didn't like him...at first. Then she realized that he had some money and was all too willing to spend it on her.

"Oscar wasn't the typical guy that Regina would go for," Clark said. "Regina liked the 'bad boy', the thug. Oscar wasn't in street gang culture. He had immigrated from Mexico and actually had a real job, earning his living the old fashioned way as a truck driver. If anything, Regina would see someone like him as a sucker, someone who she could use."

Still, Regina was what Oscar wanted. He persisted in calling her, asking when he could see her again.

"He's a creepy guy," Regina told her sister, Margaret as her cell phone rang. She looked at the caller ID. Yep, it was Oscar.

"But maybe you can get some money from him?"

"Here, you talk to him," Regina said handing the cell phone to Margaret. "Just make up some baloney that I'm in jail or something."

"What?"

"Get rid of him. Tell him I need bail money."

"Hello, Oscar?" Margaret answered the phone.

"Yeah," Oscar said. "Who is this?"

"It's Margaret," she said, sounding as if she was trying to stifle tears. "Regina is in jail. She's locked up."

"What?"

"They put her in jail for something she didn't even do. They want one thousand dollars. One thousand dollars to bail her out."

Margaret smiled like a devil at her sister.

"I can help," Oscar said.

"No," Margaret said, sniffling. "It's too much."

"It's for your sister."

Oscar would persist in his willingness to help out, however. Margaret played him like a violin, agreeing to meet with Oscar to take his hard earned money.

"Oscar gave Margaret the money in the hopes of scoring points with the sisters," Clark said. "He thought that by being 'nice' and bailing them out of trouble they would find him attractive. Instead, it just fueled their contempt for him. These girls liked thugs. Bums. They cared little for Oscar's chivalry."

Regina would not use the money to pay back her mother, however. She would give the money to her real boyfriend, Johnny, who bought an "old school ride" car with Oscar's money.

Oscar would call Regina over twenty-four times during the next five days wanting to know what happened. He began to feel like the sucker he was.

He had a wife and kids in Mexico. But here in Chicago he fell for the brown-haired beauty and became all too willing to be her patsy.

"Oscar was playing with fire," Clark said. "He just didn't realize how far gone the girls were in terms of narcissism. He didn't see the fact that they didn't even see him as a human being. All he saw was batting eyelashes and pretty faces. He was totally smitten with Regina despite the fact that he had a wife and kids back in Mexico. Here he was, in Chicago, where he was free from the responsibilities of family. He could have a little fun and if he had to spend some money to do it, so be it."

CHAPTER THREE

The two sisters were surprised at how easy it was to extract money out of Oscar. With one fake phone call, they had one thousand dollars cash to their name.

"They were both attractive girls in the neighborhood," Clark said. "They were young, looking up to gang members and drug dealers for the power they had. But the girls realized that they had their own power. The power of budding sexuality that could make men do what they wanted. They could trick men into doing things for them with a future promise of sex."

Oscar continued to call and it would be only a matter of time before he would be confronted with the truth that he had been lied to. The girls had to construct a plan to get rid of him.

"I have an idea," Margaret said, picking up the cell phone and calling their fifteen year old friend, Veronica Garcia.

"Need your help," Margaret said as Veronica picked up.

"For what?" Veronica asked.

"I need a gun. Can you get a gun?"

"A gun?"

"Can your boyfriend get a gun?"

Veronica, like the DeFrancisco sisters, was enamored with street gang members. She had a boyfriend who could obtain whatever you needed, drugs or guns.

"Why?"

"We're going to stick up and rob Oscar," she said.

"You're not going to kill him are you?"

"We're just going to scare him a little," Margaret laughed.

Veronica did as she was asked, getting a gun from her boyfriend and heading straight over to the DeFrancisco sister's home.

"Nice," Margaret said, looking the pistol over, closing one eye as she looked through the cross hairs. "So where we going to do this?"

"Right here," Regina said, waving her hands around the living room.

"No way," Margaret said. "If the neighbors complain about us screaming and yelling then they're going to hear a gunshot. Duh."

Regina looked around the home. The basement door caught her eye.

"We'll lead him down there," Regina said, leading her sister down the basement steps. "Nobody can hear anything down here. The noise will be drowned out."

"Here," Margaret said, removing some blue tarp from the shelf. She spread the material down on the basement floor in front of the steps. "We can't leave any blood stains."

"Check you out," Regina laughed. "Miss Perry Mason."

Margaret laughed as she flattened out the tarp, placing it in a perfect line with the basement stairs. "Okay," she said, walking halfway up the steps. "So if we shoot him from here," pointing her forefinger into a gun. "He'll fall straight down there."

"Perfect."

The two sisters giggled and gave each other fist bump.

"Here is where the disconnect took place," Clark said. "They had embraced an environment and a culture where there were a lot of faux tough guys. Guys who said they would commit violence but for the most part it was all talk. The girls took it literally. At no point did they realize the gravity of what they were doing. They wanted to be 'gangstas', they wanted to be seen as 'hard'. They didn't have the maturity or the experience to realize that all of those 'gangstas' that they look up to are in jail. They didn't see Oscar at all. He was less than human. Something that is used, discarded and desecrated when it is no longer of use."

CHAPTER FOUR

Oscar was surprised that Regina finally called him back.

"Hey," she said, her teenaged voice soft and inviting.

"You're out of jail?" he asked.

"Yeah," she said. "I really appreciate what you did for me. That was really sweet of you."

"No worries," he said. "I need my money back. Been calling you like crazy."

"I'm sorry, I've just been busy."

"Yeah, I understand. But I need my money back."

"I was wondering if there was some other way I can pay you back?" she said in a sensual tone of voice.

"Like?"

"Like, I know you think my sister is hot, right?"

"What's that got to do with anything?"

"It is something we've been thinking about," she said. "But if you're not cool with it, it's okay."

"Not cool with what?"

"We were wondering if," Regina giggled. "If you can come over for a threesome."

Oscar couldn't believe his luck. He had heard of white girls being freaky, he just didn't think he would ever be able to experience it himself.

Naive to their plan, he rushed over and parked his car outside their mother's home in the South Side of Chicago.

He knocked on the door and was greeted by Margaret and Veronica Garcia, a friend of the two sisters. He didn't see the .38 caliber semi-automatic pistol had in her back waistband.

"Does anyone else know you're coming over?" Margaret asked.

"No," Oscar mumbled, shrugging his shoulder.

Margaret nodded her head and let the young man in. He saw Regina step into the room holding a bin of dirty laundry.

An awkward silence ensued followed by even more awkward smiles. The two sisters fed off each others willingness to go through with the plan. Even if one of them had second thoughts, they would be deemed "soft" by the other.

They had to go through with the murder.

Both women looked over at the young man with come hither looks. Regina said nothing as she opened the basement door and walked down.

"You go with Regina," Margaret said smiling.

"Right," Oscar said, his heart pounding in anticipation as he followed her down.

Oscar heard Margaret's footsteps behind him. What he didn't know was that she had a gun pointed at the back of his head.

When he reached the bottom step, she pulled the trigger.

The young man died instantly, falling face first in the tarp.

"Holy shit!" Margaret said. "I had no idea it would be that fucking loud. It doesn't sound that loud on TV."

Margaret came down the stairs. She kicked Oscar in the head hard, sending more blood spraying across the floor and wall.

"Nobody heard," Regina said as she knelt down and began rifling through Oscar's pockets.

"What the fuck was that?" Veronica said, calling down from the top of the basement steps.

"Did you see that? " Margaret asked. "He fell down like a baby!"

The sisters took out his wallet which had over $600 cash. They took his cell phone then ripped off the sterling silver chain from his neck.

"What the fuck happened?" Veronica said, her voice trembling as she came down a few steps.

"We shot his ass," Margaret said. "He's dead. Look at that shit, he's bleeding through his ears."

"Why did you do it?" Veronica screamed. "Why? Oh my God!"

"Shut the fuck up!" Margaret screamed.

"Don't just stand there," Regina commanded. "Come and help."

Their lifelong friend could only watch as the two sisters took out his car keys and wrapped up his body in a flowery bed sheet.

CHAPTER FIVE

"The girls suffered from what I call the 'Lord of the Flies' syndrome," Clark said. "Here they are hanging out with drug dealers, obtaining guns, killing men in the basement. There is no parental figure in sight! They are left to fend for themselves and the end result is murder and mayhem."

With the dead body in the basement, both sisters peeked out their window, waiting for dark.

Confident that the entire neighborhood was asleep, they opened the door and carried Oscar's body out of the home.

The three girls struggled carrying the dead weight, wrapping his body with a comforter and the flowered bed sheet.

They opened up the trunk and placed the body inside.

"What are you guys doing?" a woman yelled from a window across the street.

The girls looked up startled.

"We're getting rid of some furniture" Regina called out. "No worries."

The girls waved at the neighbor as she moved away from the window.

"Nosy bitch," Regina whispered.

Margaret giggled. Veronica still scared, said nothing.

They got into the vehicle and drove to a vacant lot where they took out Oscar's body again.

"This is hard work," Regina complained. "Shit!"

They plopped the body on the ground, looking at it for a beat before Regina reached back into the trunk. She pulled out a bottle of nail polish remover and poured the liquid over the tarp.

"Are you sure that's gonna work?" Margaret asked.

"It says 'highly flammable'," Regina said, shrugging her shoulders.

Margaret lit a match and set the material on fire.

The flame went up immediately, the girls could feel the warmth on their faces in the cold Chicago night.

"Told you this shit would work!" Regina said.

Then as fast as the flame started, it quickly died down.

"Light another one," Regina said.

Margaret threw down another match, getting the flames going again as Regina doused the tarp with the remaining nail polish remover.

Satisfied, the girls quickly got back into the Camaro and drove off.

**

An anonymous call came into police headquarters reporting the fire in the vacant lot. The caller investigated further, however, and saw Oscar's arm sticking out through the fire. He called 911 again with a sense of urgency, telling them of the body.

CHAPTER SIX

When police on scene identified Oscar Velazquez' partially burned body, their initial knee-jerk reaction was that this was the work of a local street gang, a drug deal gone awry. But when they found the nail polish remover bottle, however, they quickly realized that this was the work of amateurs. A jealous girlfriend maybe.

Meanwhile, the DeFrancisco sisters cruised around town over the following days, trying to pawn off the Camaro.

"This is where the sisters make the guys in 'Dumb and Dumber' look like geniuses," Clark said. "They had only pre-planned the front end of the murder. Like most impulsive killers, they had no idea what to do after. Their greed took over and they decide to sell the Camaro. They have no papers for it, duh, and really can only sell a stolen vehicle to a thug. They find no takers as even the dumbest street gang member isn't going to buy a hot car from two teenaged girls. So they cruise around town and Oscar's brother spots them in the car."

The girls, failing in their sales efforts, would later abandon he vehicle behind a storefront and set it on fire.

**

The day after Oscar's killing, a mutual friend named Jessica Benitez stopped by the house. Jessica went downstairs and watched Margaret mop up a stain of blood near the basement steps.

"The hell is that?" she asked.

Margaret said nothing as she poured bleach over the blood, scrubbing hard.

"Dude bled all over the floor," Regina said. "But only after Margaret kicked him in the head. We called him over, told this idiot we'd have a threesome with him. Then we robbed his ass."

"But the blood stain on the floor-" Jessica asked, watching Margaret clean up.

"We killed a guy," Margaret said without remorse.

"He was going to kill us!" Regina said. "Margaret shot him in the back of the head. We searched his body and found a gun in his waistband. Then we wrapped him up in plastic and put him in his car."

"Holy shit, girl," Jessica.

"We're about to go on the run," Margaret announced.

"Aren't you scared?" Jessica asked, looking back down at the blood stain in the basement.

"I ain't scared of nothing," Margaret said. "You should have seen his head when I shot him. His brain oozed out like cheese."

Margaret made a rolling motion with her hands.

Jessica then accompanied Margaret to the store she purchased a bottle of blonde hair dye for her "disguise."

"We see here how the whole street gang culture has influenced the behavior of these girls," Clark said. "At any point in time, Veronica or Jessica could have went straight to the police. But they get caught up in the drama of the moment. The so-called 'loyalty' to their friend who, quite frankly, would shoot them up in a heartbeat if they knew that they were going to be a snitch."

Going off the tip from Oscar's brother, the police show up to question both Regina and Margaret. The duo denied ever seeing Oscar.

They then go to interview Veronica Garcia.

They found the jittery fifteen year old to be a different story, however. The teen quickly crumbled under the pressure of questioning and told the police the entire story.

Feeling the heat, the DeFrancisco sisters go on the run...

CHAPTER SEVEN

For all of their stupidity in committing the murder, the DeFrancisco sisters deftly avoided capture for almost two years.

They decided to split up. Margaret would go to live with their maternal aunt in Roscoe, Illinois, an hour and a half drive away from where they lived. Roscoe was a small town with less then 10,000 people, a far cry from the drug infested streets of Chicago. Margaret's worst dreams were now realized. She was now a nerd who had to stay inside all day long, living in a boring cul-de-sac with no street gang action. Neighbors would remark that they would never see her and if hey did she would quickly go back inside.

Living underground without detection, it took a broadcast of the television show AMERICA'S MOST WANTED to generate an anonymous tip which led to Margaret's whereabouts. Police staked out her aunt's apartment and entered, finding Margaret in her bedroom with a blank look on her face.

"My feelings were hurt bad because she (my wife) did something behind my back," Margaret's uncle by marriage said later. "I knew (police) were going to find her anyway."

Seven months later, Regina was captured in Dallas living with her Latin King boyfriend, Johnny Rivera.

Initially, she did not even know where the gang banger lived. She just knew the town, Laredo, and she journeyed there by bus. Regina would eventually find him, locating one of his relatives. She would live under an alias and claimed that she worked as a maid.

Police knew better. Regina made money by selling drugs under the Latin King banner.

Unlike Margaret, Regina had evaded the scrutiny of the America's Most Wanted viewers.

Her capture came about because she could not stop hanging out with the wrong crowd.

Two sheriffs were had mistakenly arrived at her boyfriend's apartment, wanting to serve a warrant to someone else.

Rivera allowed the deputies to enter his apartment but he had left a marijuana flake on his table. Police searched the apartment further and found several packages of crack cocaine ready to be sold.

The deputies arrested Rivera. They searched inside the apartment and interviewed Regina, who was groggy from a cocaine high. She showed them her false Texas identification and they let her go.

But the deputies smelled something fishy on her aside from marijuana. They had the apartment manager set up a meeting with her. She arrived at the complex in an SUV with another man. The police approached and the SUV sped away.

The high-speed chase down residential Dallas streets reached upwards of 90 mph. The SUV then slammed into a center median, the front tires blowing out.

Regina got out of the car and tried to sprint away. A deputy tackled her and they fell to the ground, her cell phone skidding across the gravel road. Sifting through her pockets, the officer found over $1,500 cash.

She was taken to Dallas County Jail where they discovered her true identity.

"We pulled her out of jail," said a Deputy Dodson. "I asked to see one of her tattoos, and she showed me...I called her by name, but she never said a word to me. She knew it was over."

She was then extradited to Illinois to stand trial for the murder of Oscar Velazquez.

CHAPTER EIGHT

The trial of the two women began in July of 2004 and both sisters pleaded not guilty by reason of self-defense.

But their friend, Veronica Garcia, had cut a deal with prosecutors in return for a lesser sentence. She would provide the testimony that would damn the two sisters to prison.

Garcia said that she didn't know what the sisters had planned. She had simply provided the gun to the DeFrancisco's which she thought would be used for a robbery only.

"I didn't see her shoot Oscar," Veronica said.

The prosecution brought forth additional witnesses in Jessica Benitez, Luciana Macias, and Maria Constantino, the neighbor.

"Both of them told me that they killed Oscar," Jessica said. "Margaret kicked him in the head so he could die faster."

"I saw them load the body into the back of the Camaro," Constantino said. "Regina told me that she planned out the killing."

Margaret, however, maintained their innocence. She said that Oscar came to the apartment angry because the sisters had tricked him out of one-thousand dollars.

"I shot him to protect Regina," Margaret said.

"Then why didn't you tell the reporting officer what happened?" the prosecution attorney asked.

"We would've got in trouble," Margaret said. "If I told the truth, I would've been there longer."

Regina DeFrancisco would also take the stand and claim self-defense as well.

"I came out of my bedroom," Regina said. "And he was there, cursing and screaming. He pulled a gun on me. I thought I was going to die. I curled up on the floor, in a fetal position. I begged for my life. Then I heard a gunshot and saw Margaret standing over Oscar, holding a gun."

"Whose idea was it to dispose of the body?"

"Veronica knew of this vacant lot," Regina said. "It was her idea."

The jury would deliberate for over six and a half hours. Regina would be found guilty of murder. Margaret's jury, however, was unable to convict her. There was and 11 to 1 deadlock with one juror believing that she should be acquitted. The juror did not believe that someone so young could commit murder.

Margaret was then released from custody and told to await retrial. She had a baby during this time, a girl, and would find work as a nursing assistant while she awaited another trial.

Four months later, Margaret would be given another day in court. Veronica Garcia would once again be the star witness for the prosecution, detailing the exact same testimony as before.

There would be no deadlock in this second go around as Margaret would be convicted of first-degree murder.

Regina would be sentenced to 35 years in prison while Margaret would be sentenced to 46 years. Both women are now jailed at the Dwight Correctional Center. They have each filed appeals which have been denied.

"The girls cared nothing about Oscar Velazquez," Clark said. "In the end, they remained true to their own narcissistic nature. They only cared about what was happening to the next. They cared about nothing about the now fatherless children Oscar Velazquez would leave behind nor about the fact that the took his life."

Veronica Garcia was jailed for five years. She served her full sentence and has since been released.

"This is a cautionary tale if there ever was one," Clark said. "The sisters had it all. They had access to one of the finest schools in their state. Yet they chose to throw it all away for short money and the cheap thrill of the 'thug life.' In the end, they got to see what the 'thug life' was really all about. Mindless violence where everyone is out for themselves, especially when there is a plea bargain to be made. They could have had it all had they stayed on the straight and narrow. Now they have nothing."

KILLER BABE : THE TRUE STORY OF BRITTANY HOLBERG

Brittany Holberg was a twenty-three years old prostitute when she was convicted of murdering 80-year-old A.B. Towery Jr, stabbing him over sixty times.

The controversy surrounding the case centered around the relationship of Brittany and Towery prior to the killing. Brittany argued that Towery was a client who went into a rage when he found drugs on her person. He attacked her and she retaliated in self-defense.

Further investigation would reveal otherwise, however, as Brittany would use numerous household items in a brutal assault on the elderly man.

She fled the scene only to be caught at a McDonald's after police received a tip from a witness who saw her on "America's Most Wanted."

With her good looks and well-proportioned body, Brittany has remained in the spotlight as she was featured in a Maxim Magazine article as one of the "hottest women on death row".

Brittany still sits on death row today with her case being appealed on the numerous levels in the court system.

EARLY LIFE

Brittany was born on January 1, 1973, in Amarillo, Texas.

Accounts on Brittany's home life vary as she would manipulate according to the needs of her listener. To her probation officer, she informed them that her home life was "good" and that she "had everything that she ever wanted". She would often describe her mother as her best friend.

During other occasions, however, Brittany would paint a different story.

She would describe her parents as being "hippie-drugsters". Brittany would state that she was close to her mother but never knew her father, a heroin addict who was in and out of the Texas prison system. Her mother would later marry a man named John Schwartz with the couple marrying and divorcing four times.

They would drink heavily and openly smoke weed in front of the young Brittany who would be sexually assaulted by a babysitter at the age of five. When she was twelve, one of her aunts was murdered and according to Brittany "everything fell apart" at home. Her parents would leave her unattended as they indulged in pot and booze.

"They just stopped working," Brittany said. "They just let everything go."

She would be gang raped by two men who confronted her in an alley behind her home when she was thirteen.

Brittany would then spend the majority of her time living with her grandmother. By the age of sixteen, however, she would run away with her boyfriend Ward. The two would make it as far as California, get married, and have a young daughter named Mackenzie.

The union would not last long, however. Brittany would divorce Ward and move back to her native Amarillo. Ward would take Mackenzie and move to Tulsa, Oklahoma.

Brittany would state that she suffered a knee injury and would become addicted to pain medication during treatment. She would then graduate to harder drugs like cocaine.

In and out of rehab, Brittany's life spiraled out of control. She could manipulate with the best of them, however, and would escape from the Midland Halfway House with the help of a female counselor.

Brittany would hang out with the drug-using crowd and her own habits were out of control. To support her addiction, Brittany began working as a prostitute.

This would put her in harm's way on many an occasion as she would get gang-raped and beaten severely.

The assault would put her in the hospital but she would resume "tricking" when she was released.

"At that point in her life, Brittany was incorrigible," forensic psychologist Paula Orange said."Numerous people had reached to her and tried to help. She had extended family members trying to help. Friends trying to help. Even church outreach workers. All to no avail. The drugs had taken root and she was dead set on manipulating everyone around her. Family, roommates, church members, doctors, dentists, and pharmacists would all fall victim to her schemes to get drugs."

By 1993, Brittany was a full-blown drug-addicted prostitute with the rap sheet to prove it. In April of that year, she would steal a gun from her step-father. She then passed over $1300 in "hot" checks and applied for several store credit cards using a fake name.

Brittany and one of her aunts would run a scam on dentists, lying to them about their pain levels in order to get prescription medication. When the prescription drugs ran out, she would return to street drugs like cocaine and heroin. Arrests would follow and Brittany would be charged in Hale County with drug possession, paraphernalia, and public intoxication.

Upon her release, Brittany would proceed to steal her mother's car and forge checks in her name. The prostitution continued unabated as well as she stole the wallet from one of her "tricks" who pressed charges.

While in jail for the theft, Brittany would be introduced to Ella Gibbs and Patricia Karnes who ran the ministry in the Randall County Jail. The women tried to get Brittany on the right track and introduce her to Christianity.

"I wanted to reassure Brittany that she is a valuable person, that her life has great potential, and that this is the mortal portion of an eternal life," Karnes said. " Brittany is an eternal being and through the many prayers from my [prayer] group [in Lubbock,] I have been led to come back into this child's life to support her here, to encourage her, to find her courage from the Holy Spirit within her, and to let her know that there is a human being mortal person who will stand beside her and see the good in her and support whatever God plans for the rest of your [sic] life."

A.B. TOWERY

Towery was by all accounts a nice man. His son would bristle at the idea that he was Brittany's "sugar daddy".

"Dad wasn't a dirty old man," his son said. "Dad was just trying to help somebody and look what he got, and now she's getting three meals a day and a warm place to sleep."

The defense would later bring up the fact that he once pulled a knife on his son Russell during a temper tantrum. Towery would have a history with prostitutes (according to court testimony). Connie Baker would be a prostitute from the 1980s to 1997 and stated that Towery was one of her clients. Baker would also claim Tower as a client but she also had a history of drug possession and auto theft. Diana Wheeler would also admit to being one of Towery's prostitutes in the years of 1994 and 1995. She had come to his home and he even went so far as to clean the stains off his Mel Mac dinnerware. But Wheeler also had a long criminal history like Baker, arrested for prostitution, criminal trespass and giving false identification to a police officer.

The controversy at the trial was if Brittany and Towery had an ongoing "sex-for-money" relationship.

This would be vigorously discounted by family members.

His daughter-in-law would come to the home and help with some housekeeping. His sons would also visit daily and never report any "ladies of the evening" coming to visit their father.

The picture just didn't fit.

Brittany stated she was sent to Towery's place by a fellow streetwalker who went by the moniker of "Green Eyes" but that it was later revealed that no such prostitute by that name existed. Brittany had lied like she had so many times before.

The two seemed to have met by chance.

COMING BACK FROM THE GROCERY STORE

November 13th, 1996 was another normal day for the 80-year old A.B Towery. He had just purchased groceries at an Albertson's store and was walking back to his apartment. As he entered the courtyard, he was approached by the 23-year old Brittany Holberg.

She asked to use his telephone and Towery consented. He wanted to help the sweet-voiced Brittany and didn't believe that she posed any kind of physical threat to him.

What he didn't know was that Brittany was coming down from a cocaine high and had not slept in ten days.

"Brittany could be persuasive," Orange said. "She was well-versed in how to charm people, she knew exactly what to say and do in terms of body language. She was like a trained actress. It didn't take much cajoling on her part to convince Towery to let her inside his home. He probably thought 'what's the big deal?'"

Once inside, Brittany would demand money from the elderly man but he refused. Brittany then attacked Towery, trying to strong arm the wallet out of his pocket. The struggle began in the living room. The two then pushed and pulled each other around a partition that separated the kitchen from the living room. They then returned to the living room. At some point, Towery tried to leave the apartment but Brittany pulled him back in. The evidence also indicated that the two paused during this 45-minute fight, catching their breath and nursing their wounds. Brittany would sustain minor stab wounds to her stomach and thigh.

"This was most likely a fight that had a lot of clutching and grabbing," Orange said. "There was less blood in the living room so the conjecture is that is where the fight started. There was blood near the door so that suggests that Towery was bleeding out and trying to escape for help. Remember, he was a slow-moving 80-year old man. Brittany was a young woman but she was fueled by cocaine. He's getting tired a lot faster than she will."

Eventually, Brittany gained the upper hand. She used various objects around the home to beat down Towery. She started with a cast iron frying pan, then a steam iron, a claw hammer, a fruit knife, a butcher knife and then two forks. Towery would fall to the floor, a bloody mess.

Brittany then took a lamp and shoved its base five inches down his throat which choked him to death.

Satisfied that he had finally killed Tower, Brittany removed her bloody clothes. She washed up in his bathroom then went to his closet to find some clothes that fit her.

Walking back to his dead body, Brittany retrieved the wallet out of Towery's pocket. She took out the $1400 dollars he had and dropped the now empty wallet onto his stomach.

Brittany casually walked out of the apartment and hitched a ride with a young couple. The couple dropped her off at a local crack house where Brittany paid them off with two $100 bills (which had blood stains on them). Inside the drug den, Brittany befriended the proprietor and changed clothes again. She then went to a local hotel with hundreds of dollars worth of cocaine and indulged.

TRIAL

Brittany's defense attorney, Catherine Brown Dodson, would argue that Holberg acted in self-defense when she killed Towery. Her primary argument was that Towery was far from an innocent, elderly man. He was, in fact, a drug abuser himself who became physically violent with Brittany when he found a crack pipe on her person. He then hit Brittany two times in the head when she turned her back to him. Brittany retaliated and ultimately put the lamp post in his mouth in an attempt to end the fight.

Brittany then fled as she believed that no one would believe her side of the story because she was both a prostitute and a drug addict.

While in jail, Brittany would try to coerce Katina Dixon, her cellmate to kill Vickie Marie Kirkpatrick who was the prosecution witness.

Towery's history with prostitutes would be brought up in court testimony. They would also mention incidents of violence with his ex-wife and children but jurors didn't believe the old man was in any type of shape to employ the service of a prostitute.

"My father didn't even like the word 'sex'", one of his sons said. "He was old-fashioned."

A psychiatrist would testify, however, that Brittany had battered wife syndrome, post-traumatic stress disorder, and cocaine addiction.

The jury did not take long to deliberate, finding Brittany to be a cunning, manipulative liar who committed one of the most brutal crimes in the history of Amarillo.

They would find her guilty and Brittany would be moved to death row at Gatesville, Texas.

"I can't even explain to you," Brittany said in a magazine interview. "What it's like to have someone say 'You are sentenced to die.' It's words. You feel helpless, numb. It's almost as if your emotions shut you down."

Brittany would spend her first few weeks in prison laying prone on her bed in a zombie-like state. Over time, she grew accepting of her situation. She knew she was going to die but made it a point to learn to take each day one step at a time.

Her inspiration for cleaning up her act came from the memory of her daughter Mackenzie.

"I cannot live," Brittany said. "And I cannot die, knowing that my child has to live with the horror that these people tried to say about me, the story of the crime, their depiction that I was a cold-blooded person."

Brittany states that she dedicates her days to reading, writing to family and working on her law appeals. She also is anti-death penalty advocate.

She would follow other Texas inmates who were now on death row and make appeals on their behalf, specifically that of Betty Lou Beets.

"I realized," Brittany said. "It doesn't matter whether I'm guilty or innocent, this has now become a very political thing... At this point, they're just killing to kill."

She complained that after a recent jail uprising, the treatment of death row inmates has worsened.

"You would not believe the treatment we are given," Brittany said. "Just two weeks ago, we were informed that not only would we be strip-searched for our one hour of recreation a day, but also when taken for a shower. So for the last two weeks, we have been stripped no less than six times a day. This is every day, sometimes at times like 2:30-3 a.m., and we never leave the building or our cells for that matter."

As of this writing, Brittany's stay of execution has been appealed and appealed for the past eighteen years.

Her attorneys would exhaust the appeal process in the state system but it is now in the federal courts.

Her case, however, has been costing taxpayers "conservatively to be at least $400,000" according to county criminal attorney James Farren. In the future, he has decided to forgo seeking the death penalty in capital cases.

Farren continues to favor a death penalty but only under certain circumstances like "a guy walks into a day care center and kills the children or if someone kills a police officer or a firefighter in the line of duty."

Farren predicted that Brittany would remain on death row for another five years at least. "They can go through the U.S District Court in Amarillo, then it can go to the Fifth U.S Circuit Court and the U.S. Supreme Court. Then from there it can go back to the U.S. District."

But the appeals can come to a halt if the district judge refuses to hear it again.

"If the Supreme Court says 'no,'" Farren said. "That's when the district judge can feel safe in stopping this process."

The entire process has been an infuriating one for the Towery family. His son both rages and mourns about what happened to his father.

"She tried to apologize to us during the trial," Russel Towery said. " I got up and walked out. I'm sure other families are going through the same things I'm going through. It's been almost 19 years ... people forget."

"I don't want to die before she does. I want to stand there as she's kicking and screaming going to the death gurney. I want her to think about what my dad went through when she didn't even know his name," he said. "She thinks that because she said she was sorry, that everything's all right. ... she is evil and needs to be destroyed."

HUSBAND KILLER : THE TRUE STORY OF TRACEY GRISSOM

97

Claiming to be a victim of rape and other abuses, a distraught Tracey Grissom would travel to her ex-husband Hunter's workplace and shoot him six times in the back, receiving a twenty-five-year life sentence for his murder.

Her defense attorney would argue that Tracey was motivated by post-traumatic stress disorder caused by her Hunter's constant abuse and sexual assaults. One jury member had even asked the judge to be lenient in her sentencing as they were not allowed to hear details of her Hunter's alleged abuses (beatings, rape, sodomy).

But what really happened in the years that led up to May 15th, 2012? Was she in fact the victim of years of abuse by a psychotic husband? Or did she want to cash in on his $100,000 life insurance policy?

INSTANT ATTRACTION

The couple would meet during a dinner party in 2003 in Tuscaloosa, Alabama. Tracey was twenty-one years old and going through a divorce. She had a son, James Michael, from the previous marriage.

Family and friends would describe the union as "love at first sight." Hunter was blown away by the young Tracey's blue eyes and facial beauty.

"For him, it was love at first sight," crime author William Phelps said. "She was gorgeous."

A whirlwind courtship would ensue and the couple would elope in 2004.

"In the beginning, it was good," Tracey told CBS' 48 hours. "We had a friendship. Just your normal, honeymoon phase marriage."

"He was fun," Tracey said. "And he was attractive."

Hunter was two years younger than Tracey, however, and his mother felt that he had jumped the gun too early in the relationship.

Her words proved to be prophetic as after only eight months into the marriage, the marriage went south.

According to Tracey, their marital problems began with Hunter's drug addiction.

"I had caught him smoking marijuana," Tracey said. "Doing illegal things could cause a problem and I couldn't risk losing my son over."

Tracey claimed that she threatened her new spouse with a divorce but Hunter gave her his word that he would stop with his drug use. She stated that the relationship improved and the decided to start a construction company together.

"I took out an equity line to start a company," Tracey said. "Which was Grissom Construction. It was all in my name."

Hunter specialized in building elaborate boat docks. He had an artistic eye and could do docks, stairs, and other accouterments. The business began to grow in short order.

"They're going to take on the world," Phelps said. "They're going to be entrepreneurs and they're gonna make it."

They then had a daughter of their own, Anna Grace. The child was a long time coming for the couple. They had been trying for a long time as Tracey had five miscarriages before Anna Grace was born.

"She was premature," Tracey recalled. "Her heart and lungs were not developed. A very stressful time."

Behind closed doors things were rocky. On the surface, however, things looked good. They had a young family and were making money.

"All-American family," Phelps said. "White-picket fence. The whole nine yards. Middle-class. Suburbia. Maybe the Prince Charming that she's been waiting for."

But again, this was only on the surface. Tracey harbored secrets of her own. One of which was her own addiction to prescription drugs.

"Psychologically, there's something going on here," Phelps said. "There's something going on behind those beautiful eyes and it ain't good."

Tracey would often turn on on the children, showing off her temper. Then she would turn on Hunter.

"This would cause friction in the marriage," Phelps said. "And where there's friction, there's fire."

SETTING THE STAGE

Tracey would later state that Hunter would "act strangely" shortly before she filed divorce. She was a registered nurse and gave him an over-the-counter drug test. According to her, Hunter tested posted for marijuana, Oxycontin, opiates, and methamphetamine.

Hunter would later be arrested for marijuana possession but his family would insist that he never did the harder drugs.

Tracey would file for divorce in the summer of 2010 after six years of marriage. According to her, this would prompt physical abuse from Hunter.

Hunter had to move out but their divorce agreement would allow him access to the home.

"In September of 2010," Tracey recalled. "That was the first time he physically hit me. It (the abuse) got progressively worse. He had made the comments that if I told anybody he would kill me. I believed him."

Hunter' co-workers and family members would have a different take on the situation, however. His co-workers remembered a time when she tracked him down at one of the jobs and made a scene.

"She's screaming, jumping on him," Hunter's co-worker said. "Said something about him having another girlfriend and used the expression about, 'You are mine. I'll kill you. I'll kill you. You are mine."

"She's borderline demonic," Hunter's mother said. " mean, I absolutely believe—that she is that troubled."

Hunter's family continued to believe that he did not abuse Tracey.

"He did not have an abusive, an angry bone in his body," Hunter's aunt Gina said. "In fact, we kind of laughed at him because he was too laid-back."

The divorce was finalized in October of 2010.

EVIDENCE OF ABUSE?

Loran Richards was the first of Tracey's friends to notice the minor injuries on her body. She would inquire about the bruises but the answers she received were always evasive. Seeing Tracey with a black eye, however, forced her to try and get more answers.

"I said, Tracey, you may have terrible luck," Richards recalled. "But nobody is so unlucky that they trip, fall down the stairs, and hit their face on a baseball in the eye socket. So don't give me a lame excuse. You don't have to give me any excuse, but let's take a picture."

Tracey broke down. She gave her friend all of the grisly details, detailing the abuse she suffered at the hands of Hunter. Loran then became her advocate, taking pictures of Tracey's injuries. She would later state that she saw blood stains and other signs of abuse at Tracey's home.

THAT FATEFUL NIGHT

Now divorced, Hunter would arrive at Tracey's home on November 22nd, 2010.

According to Tracey, he then became enraged when Tracey told him that she had spent the night with a new lover.

"He told me that he was gonna kill me," Tracey recalled. Tracey stated that she tried to escape, running into the closet in order to "get away from the kids and to pray." Tracey's eleven-year-old son from a previous relationship was in the home as was the four-year-old daughter they have together.

Hunter caught up with her and knocked her to the ground. He tied a belt around her ankles and then began choking her.

Half-conscious, Tracey alleged to have been raped and sodomized.

The brutal attack would leave Tracey unconscious. She would wake up the next morning on the bathroom floor.

"I called Hunter," Tracey recalled. "I told him that I was bleeding and that I was hurt and that I needed help. And he told me, 'Fuck you. I hope you die."

Tracey wound up in the emergency room after the attack. Hospital records would show that she had a laceration on her head, bruises, and ligature marks on her feet.

Tracey would then be referred to the Turning Point domestic violence center.

Marian Waters would describe Tracey's injuries as among the worst she had ever seen in a twenty-year career.

Waters would testify that Tracey had suffered a horrific assault. She described her mental state as typical of someone who had just been raped; fearful, jumpy, fearing for her life.

Tracey had suffered a hematoma on her side that was the side of a grapefruit. She also claimed to have experienced rectal nerve damage which would require surgery as well as torn vaginal muscles requiring her to have a hysterectomy.

Police were called and Hunter would be arrested for rape, sodomy, kidnapping and domestic violence.

"And at that point, I feared for my life," Tracey recalled. "And I feared for my children's life."

A HIDDEN AGENDA

Hunter would be freed on bail but Tracey got a restraining order against him. She bought a gun and did not go anywhere unarmed.

She took photos of her injuries on the night of the alleged attack and texted them to Loran. Later, they would take more pictures.

Angered, Hunter would stop paying her spousal and child support. Tracey, however, may have had another scenario in mind for obtaining money.

She had forced Hunter to take out a $103,000 life insurance policy around the time their daughter was born.

On May 24, 2012, the day before Tracey shot Hunter, she would place a call to MetLife that was recorded.

"Thank you for calling MetLife, this is Pam. May I please have your name?"

"Tracey Grissom."

Tracey would then explain that she was angry that her husband stopped making payments on his policy. During their divorce proceedings, he had agreed to continue paying the premiums. Tracey stated she was calling to make sure that they had the correct address on file.

"Is there anything else I can do for you today?

"That's gonna be it!" Tracey said, hanging up.

"Well, May 14th was just like any other day," Tracey said, explaining the call to the insurance company. "However, I had moved four different times. Me and my children were running. We were running from Hunter. So I had called the company to let them know that they had my old address and to make an address change."

FALSE RAPE?

Shelly Standridge was hired by Hunter to defend him in the rape case. She would state that Hunter denied raping or even assaulting Tracey that night. Hunter did, however, admit to the fact that he and his wife had consensual sex that night...Rough consensual sex.

"So that night," Standridge said. "Hunter said that she was depressed and claiming she was going to kill herself. She was saying she wanted their relationship to work."

So she undressed in front of him. Her beauty was always impossible for Hunter to resist.

The two had sex despite Hunter having a new girlfriend at home.

Hunter's aunt, Gina, believed that Tracey wanted to kill Hunter before the rape case went to court.

"He had a new girlfriend, he was living with her," Phelps said. "He was moving on with his life. Hunter would claim that Tracey was jealous, obsessive, even stalked them."

"Hunter had moved on," Hunter's aunt said. "There was some court dates coming up that would prove that Hunter was innocent. There were court dates coming up that he would get visitation to his daughter. She had a lot to lose."

Tracey was on the anti-anxiety drug Klonopin. Hunter would tell his attorney that Tracey would take more than her prescribed dose. Because of this, she fell and cut her head. Hunter would then leave the house around 10:30 pm and go to his father's house. Tracey would call him hours later, at 3:20 am.

Hunter would state that Tracey had called to threaten him. She told him if he didn't want the responsibility of the children then she would make it where he would never be able to see them again.

Hunter's attorney did not know what Tracey's motive was for crying rape. She was very upset that he had a girlfriend.

MORE LIES...

Hunter would be arrested nearly twelve hours later, to his total shock.

Tracey would give her side of the story to the police which later is proven to be false.

She would tell police that Hunter had thrown her against the bathtub around 10 pm and claim to be unconscious until 4 am the next morning.

"But her phone records show she was on the phone all night, so she was never unconscious," Standridge said. "She was also using her data at 10:42 that night. She was using it again at 10:50 that night. ... She sends a text to her boyfriend at 1:49 am. She sends a text to her friend at 2:07 am. She sends another text to her boyfriend at 2:07 am."

Tracey would blame the calls on Hunter.

"All I do know is I was not the only person using my phone that night," Tracey said, suggesting that Hunter used her phone.

Medical records would show that Tracey's head wound was "purely superficial".

Only one suture was needed.

Furthermore, there was nothing on the medical record to support the fact that Tracey experienced vaginal and rectal tears. She did have bruises on her ankle and legs but the photos taken by police at the emergency room would not resemble the same photos that Tracey and her friend Loran would take days later. In the photos taken at the emergency room, an area of Tracey's body has no bruises. Days later, there is discoloration.

Tracey's attorney would blame the discrepancy on "blood thinners" which would cause Tracey to bruise easily.

There was also a discrepancy in her phone records. She would take a photo of her inner thigh, a deep bruise. This area of her body was not photographed by police during her emergency room visit. But on December 9th, almost two weeks later, Tracey took a photo of her inner thigh with the deep bruise

"He (Hunter) told me that he would make it to where nobody would ever want me," Tracey said after a 2010 attack. "I didn't report it because I thought he would kill me."

THE FINAL STRAW

Tracey woke up pissed on May 15th, 2012.

Hunter had been ordered to pay $2,100 a month for the rest of his life. He was not complying with the court order claiming that he was "out of work."

Tracey stated that she was on her way to a job interview when she saw a Grissom Construction sign out of the corner of her eye.

She stated that her initial plan was to take a photograph of Hunter at the job site in order to show proof that he was working as part of her litigation.

"I was getting ready to take the picture and when I looked up he was standing almost directly towards the front of the boat trailer," Tracey said. "He was looking back directly at me. He had this face, that's like mean - just, I don't know how to describe it. I mean, I see it over and over like it's right there all the time. He flipped me the bird, which to me was kinda like, 'Yeah I'm workin. Screw you.' And at that point, I panicked. At that point, I didn't know what else to do except to defend myself."

Tracey started firing. The first shot hit Hunter in the arm. He started to run and she fired again repeatedly. One of the bullets punctured Hunter's heart and he died of massive internal bleeding.

William Dockery was working with Hunter and was an eyewitness to the shooting. Hunter had turned to Dockery before the shooting and told him to "call the law". Before Dockery could pick up his cell phone, Tracey had commenced shooting.

Tracey then pulled out her own cell phone and called the cops on herself. She tearfully described that she had just murdered her husband.

CONFESSION

Tracey told detectives exactly what was going through her mind when she came upon Hunter at the construction site.

"Tell me about what happened," the detective said. "What led up to...what's going on."

"In November of 2010, he beat me unconscious and raped me...and, and left me for dead....and, and I finally pressed charges against him and he told me that he would make my life a living hell...and that's what he's done."

"What, what happened this morning that led up to you going..."

"I was going to work and I saw him...and he's been claiming that he-he's not working. And, so I pulled in there to take a picture of him...cause it was the truck that's still in my name...and the boat that's still in my name...and the trailer that's still in my name...He just stared at me and flipped me off...and I just went in there and shot him...I just shot him, I shot him, and I shot him."

Tracey would be distraught and tearful during her interrogation room confession. A few weeks later, however, she would call the insurance company to let them know that Hunter had died.

"Well, I was actually calling because I didn't know what I needed to do ... Hunter passed away May 15th and I actually am going a court case right now because it was due to self-defense..."

Hunter's family went ballistic over this. Tracey would claim that she had no money but she continued to pay his life insurance premiums.

"Even through the times when she's screamin' that she's destitute and has no money ... she continued to pay life insurance premium," Hunter's mother said.

"I don't think my sister concocted a story," Tracey's sister said. "Just so she could get insurance money. ... But that's all they (the prosecution) had."

THE TRIAL

Tracey's allegations of rape and sodomy would not be allowed in court testimony. She was allowed, however, to detail the effects of Hunter's abuse on her were.

Taking the stand, Tracey would lift up her shirt in court and show herself wearing a colostomy bag. She stated that she had undergone several surgeries after her husband's daily rapes wherein she suffered permanent rectal and vaginal damage.

Hunter's family was then allowed to speak at the hearing.

"This tremendous loss has changed me," Hunter's mother, Melanie Garner said. "And I don't know how to change back."

Chloe, Hunter's sister, had a victim's services officer read her letter in court.

"Tracey is psychotic," Chloe wrote. "She is the most selfish person human being on this earth."

"Every mother should pray every night that your son doesn't fall in love with someone like Tracey," Hunter's aunt, Gina Grissom said. "There have been lots of allegations against Hunter. We've never believed anything that has come out of her (Tracey's) mouth."

His aunt then looked directly at Tracey.

"Hunter was proud of his name. Why would you still choose to use our name, and bring it down?" suggesting that if Tracey hated him so much why didn't she go revert to her maiden name after the divorce.

The jurors would find Tracey guilty of murder. She would be sentenced to twenty-five years in prison.

One of the jurors, Janice Kelly, would contact Grissom's attorney Warren Freeman the morning after the trial. She had remorse over her decision and said that she wouldn't have convicted her had they had the rapes and abuse allegations been introduced as evidence.

"I feel I made a mistake," Kelly said. "If I had to do it over again, we'd have had a hung jury. We didn't get her side. She did not get a fair trial."

"We voted to convict because there was no dispute that Tracey shot Hunter," the jury foreman wrote in a letter that was addressed in the courthouse. "Jurors didn't believe prosecutor claims that she did it in order to collect a life insurance policy. We felt the shooting was a crime of passion, not for financial gain and that she should be sentenced accordingly. I wish we had seen evidence of the rape allegation. We feel that she just 'lost it.'"

"It's not fair, it's not fair!" Tracey sobbed as she was led out of the courthouse and to jail.

"We think the sentencing was too harsh," Tracey's attorney Warren Freeman said. "Considering you have the foreperson of the jury actually saying, we don't feel like she should be punished according to being found guilty of murder. Let's just say that there will be a basis for a new trial, and part of it will be something that the jurors saw that they weren't supposed to see and I'm going to just leave it at that until I file my motion."

"My son died running for his life," Hunter's mother said. "I don't know what was running through his mind but I hear him say 'momma.'"

"People who think that I murdered him in cold blood," Tracey said. "Either don't know the whole story or don't know everything that's happened.

Tracey was asked on CBS' 48 hours if she regretted pulling the trigger on that fateful day.

"No," she said flatly. "Because if I hadn't I would be dead. I truly believe that."

"She has a way of making everything she does look right," Hunter's aunt, Gina scoffed.

BONUS STORY

On the surface, James and Amber Cummings had it all.

They had been married for twelve years. James had inherited millions of dollars from his father and they owned a home in the peaceful, seaside town of Belfast, Maine.

"On paper, they were a couple that looked as if they had everything," forensic psychologist Paula Orange said. "Definitely one of those cases where looks are more than deceiving. They are downright deadly."

The couple met in Fort Bragg, California. Amber was a tall brunette while James was overweight and had an awkward vibe about him.

Amber found him charming, however, and would later describe him as the "nicest guy she'd ever met." She would marry him at 19 years of age and things looked bright for the young couple until Amber got pregnant.

"That is when his personality started to change," Orange said. "He would drive away Amber's family members in California and seek to keep her isolated. This brought much consternation to Amber's side of the family, obviously. There was one heart-breaking instance where Amber's mother and sister went to a neighbor's yard just to get a glimpse of Amber's daughter riding her tricycle."

James wanted no outside influence on Amber or their daughter so he began moving the family around. They left California when Amber turned five and moved to Texas. Then they traveled the country in a motor home until 2007 when the finally settled in Belfast, Maine.

"My husband said that he hated people and that he didn't care where we moved," Amber said. "I always wanted to live in a nice, small town in Maine."

EARLY LIFE

James' life seemed to have been one of trouble even though he was born into wealth.

His father would be murdered by one of his former employees in 1997 which was preceded by James making headline news as he videotaped his own mother doing heroin.

James would have numerous run-ins with the law himself.

"He had a bunch of assault charges," Orange said. "Some were cases where he was the victim. Others were cases where he was the perpetrator. When he was the perp, his father's money always bailed him out."

According to some Internet rumors, James' father had allegedly injured himself while getting off a forklift on one of the docks in the Fort Bragg harbor, breaking his knee in the fall.

Cummings then went to a friend's house and fell to the ground outside claiming that he "tripped in a hole." James' father then sued the owners of the property and won.

"That gives you an idea of the kind of guy James' father was," Orange said. "Rumors abound on the internet and in the Fort Bragg community about how he acquired his wealth. None of it is verifiable aside from the fact that the majority of the trust is funneled through a trailer park, which is odd."

Cummings Sr. would own many businesses and it would be one of his employees, a man named Williams Vargas who would gun him down.

Vargas detonated a homemade bomb he called a "firecracker" outside Cummings' home. The disgruntled employee then panicked as one of Cummings' neighbors drove by and blocked his escape. Cummings Sr. then came out with his own gun to investigate the blast which shattered his window.

Vargas then pulled out his own gun and shot Cummings. He had been working for Cummings at the Noyo Harbor trailer park and was allowed to live there in exchange for labor. But he began having problems with other residents which he would blame Cummings Sr. for.

Cummings, 77 years old at the time of his murder, had built his wealth by running restaurants, motels, a fish-processing plant as well as trailer parks. He also owned the Depot Mall shopping center and a McDonald's restaurant.

``Jim was quite an entrepreneur. He had quite a lot of land holdings, in some key areas, really, in the harbor and other areas around,'' former City Manager Gary Milliman said.

James Jr. would be the beneficiary of his father's death. He would tell people that he made his living "selling off Texas real estate" but the truth was that he was a trust fund kid living off the businesses that his father created.

The trust fund started off by giving Jams a whopping ten million dollars a year. The funds would deplete rapidly, however, as James would have a six-year legal battle against trustees whom he thought were mismanaging the money.

His mental illness would grow worse as his finances decreased.

NEO-NAZI SYMPATHIES

"He would go on daily rants about Barack Obama," Orange said. "Which would seem harmless at first until Amber realized that James was, in fact, a white supremacist. He began spending his days hunting down rare Nazi artifacts on the Internet and purchasing them."

James had applied to the National Socialist Movement, one of the largest neo-Nazi clubs in the country. He had written numerous white supremacy organizations on-line and began to mix toxic chemicals in their kitchen sink while telling Amber about his desire to make a "dirty bomb."

James had hired a pair of contractors to paint the interior of the house. The painters would later testify to witnessing James berate his wife. He would tell the men about his guns and go on about Adolf Hitler.

Thinking he had an eager audience, James bragged about his collection of silverware and plate settings that he claimed to have been used by Hitler himself.

"Check this out," James showed a swastika flag to the painter. "This was real. Not a knock-off. They actually waved this same flag while Hitler spoke."

James would run his household as if he were Hitler himself, marching around the home wearing a black hat and uniform with a Nazi armband.

Working himself up into a Nazi-like frenzy of rage, he would then abuse Amber physically, emotionally and sexually.

"He stripped away whatever self-esteem she had," Orange said. "He had no friends himself and didn't allow her to have any either."

As the years went by, James developed paranoid schizophrenic tendencies which had given birth to ideas that grew more bizarre with time. The married couple slept in separate bedrooms and James had guns placed under both of their pillows "just in case."

On one occasion, Amber left the home for an extended period of time. James immediately became enraged upon her arrival back. He demanded to know where she was and who she was with. Amber had gone to meet with a home-schooling group which they both previously agreed would be a good idea.

James went ballistic, berating Amber and throwing his sharpened Nazi knives against the wall.

CHILD ABUSE

James did not limit his abuse to Amber. His paranoid anger soon extended to their daughter, Clara.

This became evident to Amber when their daughter had come across James' collection of Nazi knives and began examining them.

"Leave those alone!" James screamed as he ran into the room and grabbed the box of knives away from the girl. "These belonged to the Führer! The Führer!"

Amber had very little self-esteem left, but she intervened when James would physically abuse their daughter. She would throw herself between the two and take the beating herself.

This would only incite James further as the would beat Amber then march up to Clara's room and continue his abuse.

"He kept them isolated and feeling helpless," Orange said. "They tried to escape on a few occasions but he caught them, keeping them locked in the house. She thought he had some kind of superhuman power."

CHILD PORNOGRAPHY

Seeking new outlets, James' mind became so perverted that he soon began indulging in child pornography. He showed his collection to Amber who shuddered in horror.

"Which one do you like best?" he would ask his wife, pointing to a series of pictures on the scream.

In addition to the child pornography, James began teaching his daughter to see the world through his racist viewpoint.

"This is equal-opportunity hatred," he preached to his daughter. "We can hate everybody."

"He was deluded," Orange said. "He actually saw himself as the second coming of Hitler. He began seeing his daughter as his future helper, someone who would be in charge of 'reconditioning' women and children after he declared war on the United States."

James wanted to build a torture chamber in the basement of the house. He told Amber about his desire to kill people and "peel the skin off their bones." He also obsessed on the Showtime television series, "Dexter", which featured a serial killer as the protagonist. James would then take long walks around the Belfast area, daydreaming about living out his 'Dexter' fantasy.

"He constantly talked about the different ways of killing and torturing people and hiding their bodies," Amber said. "He used to say it was a need in him."

THE FINAL STRAW

"The abuse happened incrementally for her," Orange said. "It is easy to sit back and judge a person like her, saying that she should have just left. But she was like a frog in a pot of cool water before it starts to boil. The abuse started small at first then bit by bit it increased as her self-esteem diminished. But when it came to protecting her daughter, she had to act."

One December 9th, 2008, Amber Cummings finally had enough.

She got up like she normally did after another night of abuse by her husband.

"Amber discovered James messing around with the chemicals in the kitchen," Orange said. "He said that he would bury her in the backyard if he said anything."

She sent her daughter downstairs to eat breakfast while she pulled out a .45 caliber pistol from underneath her pillow.

Then she held the gun underneath her own throat.

"Amber's first thought was to kill herself," Orange said. "But then she saw her daughter's doll in the room. She shuddered to think of her daughter spending the rest of her childhood with her father as she realized that it was only a matter of time before James' obsession with child pornography would make him do something to Clara. So she had to seek an alternative course of action."

Amber would later tell court-appointed psychologists that James' infatuation with child pornography and his "sexual attraction to young girls" made her believe that he was becoming obsessed with their daughter.

Fueled by her protective maternal instinct, Amber entered the bedroom where James was sleeping. She never had any gumption to stand up for herself when James abused her.

But when it came to protecting her daughter, a whole new Amber showed up.

She pointed the gun at the back of James' head and fired. Blood splattered against the bedpost. Shocked by her own display of violence, Amber sprinted down the steps and ordered her daughter to go to her neighbor's and stay there.

"If it wasn't for my daughter, I would have committed suicide years ago," Amber said. "Some of the mental torture will never leave me the rest of my life. It was so severe, it will be with me every day."

Amber then called the police and told them what she did.

"It's hard for us to justify shooting somebody who's asleep in the bed," Sheriff Jeffrey Trafton said. "But when we arrived she looked more like a victim than a killer."

"She was in a state of shock," Orange said. "She had finally taken action to free herself from years of abuse. The state, of course, cannot let such a deed go unchecked."

A CONSPIRACY AFOOT?

As police investigated the murder scene, they discovered another James Cummings secret.

He was gathering materials to make a "dirty bomb."

Fueled by his white supremacist ideology, James planned to go to Washington, D.C for Barack Obama's presidential inauguration. Once there, he would set off his dirty bomb.

"He had all the ingredients inside the garage," Orange said. "The FBI found the instructions for the dirty bomb. There were four 1-gallon containers with uranium, thorium and beryllium powder. There were numerous other jugs which contained lithium metal, thermite, magnesium ribbon, black iron oxide and other explosive substances. James Cummings meant business and there is clear evidence he was going to follow through on his plan. Whether he could have pulled it off is another story."

Had his plan gone to fruition, James could have potentially killed hundreds of people.

Amber saved not only herself but innumerable lives by killing James herself.

"The stuff that he had wasn't dangerous," Bangor Police Chief Jeffrey Trafton said. "In its present form, it wasn't dangerous to the community. Technicians told me what you had to do, you had to get real close for a long period of time before it would have any effect as far as the radioactivity. When the stuff was found, obviously detectives from the state police came and we didn't know what it was. But there was no danger to the community. That was established fairly quickly. But my involvement since it was handed over to the state police has been little to none."

THE TRIAL

Amber would remain in a state of shock after the murder. She worried more about her daughter's well-being than her own. She was fully prepared to go to jail.

"Her mental state was still askew after she killed James," Orange said. "She probably saw prison as a welcome respite from her abusive life. She had been in 'prison' already and saw the jail system as a safe place."

Amber would plead guilty during trial proceedings. Her story would make the media rounds, however, and she soon found numerous supporters in her small Maine town. People showed up wearing "Free Amber" t-shirts.

"There was no way in hell a jury in that vicinity would have found her guilty," Orange said. "None."

Amber seemed to have found leniency on both sides of the judicial system. Her attorney and the prosecutors would come up with a plea deal which called for a sentence of up to eight years but with Amber serving no less than a year. This would be followed by six years of probation.

Her attorney then recommended to the judge that Amber spend no whatsoever behind bars while the Assistant Attorney General, Leane Zania, wanted Cummings to spend a year in jail.

"This kind of 'self-help' is severely anti-social behavior," Zania wrote. "It will be punished accordingly."

During the course of the trial, Amber would not take the stand in her defense. Three mental health experts who had counseled her after the killing all affirmed the fact that Amber had endured traumatic abuse. They advised the judge not to send her to jail.

The psychiatrists had given Amber a diagnosis of "shared psychotic disorder" which in layman's terms meant that she had absorbed some of his craziness just by being around him.

"You don't hang out by the outhouse without getting a rash," Orange said. "So that is how Amber was able to endure all of that psychological trauma. She became so desensitized to it that it became the norm after a few years."

The judge sentenced her to eight years in prison but it was a suspended sentence, allowing her to go free.

"The terrible thing is, I was forced to take the life of someone that I loved very much to save my daughter that I love very much," Amber said. "It's something that I will have to live with for the rest of my life, and it won't be easy. I'll always wonder. I'll always be looking over my shoulder, always wondering if he can come back from the dead."

In her public remarks, Amber requested that the community forgive her husband and not have any anger toward him.

"I just want to thank the community and people of Maine," Amber said after leaving the courtroom. "Because without them, I don't think my daughter and I could have made all this progress. Really, really wonderful caring people. If I was anywhere else, we wouldn't be doing this well. I believe that with all my heart."

"The people around here are pretty incredible. They gave me the benefit of the doubt, and a chance to prove myself. There was a lot of support, an unbelievable amount of support, in Belfast. People came out and took care of us and made sure we had everything we need."

Amber stated that after she shot James that she fell into a "state of shock and numbness." She would continue to dream about James, having nightmares about him choking her.

Since then, she dedicated herself to trying to undo the mental damage James did to her daughter.

"I hope to raise a really good kid, who cares a lot about people," Amber said. I hope she ends up strong and can take care of herself. I think she will."

BONUS STORY: DEATH ROW GRANNY

It never ends.

No way.

No way am I letting this man demean and degrade me another day.

He's just like my father.

A binge drinker. And the binges were happening more and more.

He's on the road to nowhere and taking me with him.

It never ends.

First my father. Now him.

Fuck it.

I threw the cigarette on the blanket. I knew it was flammable.

Then I watched the smoke rise and smiled.

In Lumberton, North Carolina, Thomas Burke fell victim to a house fire which was caused by a burning cigarette. Investigative authorities thought that he had fallen asleep while smoking, leaving thirty-eight-year-old Velma Burke as his widow.

They didn't know that the fire was set by Velma.

Velma knew how to play the part of the grieving widow. She cried and gave the authorities the requisite crocodile tears. No one would believe that the murder of Thomas Burke would set off a series of killings performed by the seemingly kind and harmless church-going woman with the soft voice.

EARLY LIFE

Velma Bullard grew up as the second of nine children in the rural part of Sampson County, North Carolina.

Times were tough for the Bullard family. They would live on a small farm with no electricity, running water or an outhouse.

"They had to go outdoors," forensic psychologist Paula Orange said. "The entire family had to endure the indignity of going into the woods or using pots to shit and piss."

The home was small and cramped for the nine children. Velma would be forced to sleep in the same bedroom with her parents until the age of five.

Her father was a loom repairman (fixing an apparatus that was used to weave clothing) and an abusive alcoholic. Velma had an older brother, Olive, who were subject to his nightly beatings. Lillie, her mother, was too meek to protect her children from her husband's violent outbursts.

"She had the type of father who would not need any provocation," Orange said. "He would take out the pettiest frustrations, like not being able to find something around the house, and take it out on the children. Velma would become resentful toward her mother who was too weak or indifferent to stop her father from beating on the kids. She accepted his discipline as 'the way it was.'"

Velma would find school as a welcome escape from her dreadful home life. She loved her teacher and was an excellent student during her early grade school years. When she would return home from school, she took solace in the fact that her father would always arrive home late as he worked long hours at the textile mill.

"Her father Murphy had that Protestant work ethic in him," Orange said. "He accepted the long hours and low pay, seeing a kind of nobility in that. Only problem was, he would binge drink. Not store bought alcohol but homemade moonshine. After a couple of shots, he would be 'lit' and inflict his wrath on everyone in the house."

By the age of eleven, Velma would be forced to take on various chores around the farm. She would clean up the house, washing and iron everyone's clothing (eleven people). Her father would chastise her for not mending or sewing his work clothes properly as well.

"Her father was a stern taskmaster," Orange said. "Hell, you can say 'slave driver.' He would have Velma come home early from school days when the laundry got too backed up. Velma hated this and felt embarrassed. Her family didn't have much and as she grew older her classmates began to see her for what she was, a poor girl that was an easy mark for teasing."

Velma would grow to be 5'3" but gain weight as she got older. She would be mocked about her obesity, her shoddy clothes the gap between her two front teeth. She would also be called "knot head" after she ran head first into a boy at school which left a permanent contusion on her forehead.

By the age of twelve, Velma seemed to have taken on all of her mother's duties. She would cook all of the family meals in addition to performing cleaning around the farm house. She would miss school for days at a time as her father forced her to complete chores around the home before she could continue her education.

"Academic achievement was not at the forefront of her father's mind," Orange said. "Her mother was of little use because of her depression and mental illness. Velma was the oldest girl so she took on the duties of mom at an age where she should have been playing with dolls."

ANGER, ABUSE, AND CHURCH

Despite her father's verbal abuse and alcohol-fueled beatings, the family kept up a face of religious interest. Velma would be sent to Bible school every year until the age of thirteen. During her last year of Bible school, her father marked the occasion by buying Velma a silk pink dress with ribbons. Velma recalled the day as one of the happiest of her life.

The happiness would be short-lived.

Velma would claim that her father raped her when she was thirteen years old. She revealed this only to her pastor in her later years before she stood trial. Velma did not even tell her mother whom she did not think would believe the molestation took place.

"Things that went on inside our home when I grew up," Velma said. "Were kept inside."

At the age of fifteen, Velma continued to excel in school. Despite her chubby physique, she becomes adept at basketball and is pegged to be the team's star player for the upcoming season. But her father did not allow her to play.

"Who is going to iron these damn clothes?" he snarled.

The family then moved to Robeson county and switched from the Presbyterian denomination to Baptist. It was here that Velma would meet Thomas Burke and the two made it clear that they wanted to date. Once again, Velma's father would intervene, telling Velma that she had to wait until her sixteenth birthday until she could date.

The two waited patiently for her birthday to arrive and the following year Thomas would propose to her while they went to the movies.

Knowing that her father would not approve, Velma and Thomas eloped, moving to Dillon, South Carolina. Neither Thomas or Velma had any money as they both quit high school to get married. Thomas then went to work at a local textile mill.

"At this point, I believe that Velma began to realize that her life would not be that much better with Thomas," Orange said. "He literally has the same job as her father."

Economics forced Velma and Thomas to move in with his parents. This arrangement would last for a year until Thomas got a better paying job at a soft drink company.

At the age of nineteen, Velma would give birth to her first son, Ronnie. The couple would then move back to Parkton, North Carolina where they would remain in the same home for eleven years. Two years later, the young couple would welcome a daughter named Kim.

A CYCLE OF RELIGION AND ABUSE

The Burkes would be fixtures at the local Baptist church with Velma taking the reigns to teach a Sunday school class. But the prayers and sermons would do little to offset the growing ennui in the Burke home. Two years after giving birth to Kim, Velma would get hit by a drunk driver while crossing the street. She would be hospitalized for an extended period, suffering both physically and mentally.

Thomas' job at the soft drink company would not be enough to provide for the family. Velma would be forced to leave her small children at home and work in a textile mill just like her father. The couple would have different work hours, with Velma working nights and Thomas working days as they would take turns watching the children.

Velma would fall victim to the hard work at the mill and the stress of raising two young children. She began bleeding and her doctor performed a hysterectomy.

Velma's mother would take pity on the couple and give them one acre of land near their old farm. Thomas would build a three-bedroom home for the family but Velma was already going down a slippery slope. Her personality changed after the hysterectomy, claiming that she always felt "nervous and afraid."

Things would get worse as Thomas suffered a head injury in a car accident. He then began to drink heavily and begin to beat Velma.

"It was deja vu," Orange said. "Velma had, in essence, married her father."

One night, the couple argued and Thomas punched Velma in an alcohol-fueled tantrum. The police are called to the home and Velma sent Thomas to the state hospital to get treatment for his drinking. Her husband remains there for three days but when he returns home, his behavior is worse than behavior. He's angry at Velma for sending him to the "drunk tank". His alcoholism worsens and he would go on to lose his job because of absenteeism.

"Velma is thirty-five years old at this time," Orange said. "But she's an old thirty-five with crow's feet under her eyes and a hangdog look. She's had a rough life, not necessarily by her own design, and it has taken its toll."

Velma leaves the textile mill but then finds two different jobs in order to support the family. During the day, she works as a sales clerk in a Belk department store. At night, she goes to work as a machine operator in a cotton mill.

Thomas, meanwhile, would continue to drink.

He rages on a daily basis, on one occasion he pinned son Ronnie up against the wall and threatened him with a knife. Velma would faint during the encounter and be transported to the hospital. She was diagnosed as having a nervous breakdown and lapsed into a serious depression. The medical staff gave her tranquilizers to calm down. Velma believed that it was during this stint in the hospital that she became addicted to the painkillers.

"The drugs were helping," Orange said. "When nothing else did. So she wanted more and more."

Velma's children acknowledged that their mother's mood swings were due to the drugs.

Over the next three years, Velma would go in and out of the hospital for drug overdoses. After each visit, her addiction only grew as did her prescription list.

"She fell through the cracks in her own family," Orange said. "And in the system itself. Her family had their own issues to deal with as Thomas would abuse everyone on a daily basis. Finally, Velma did something she could control. She killed her husband."

On April 21st, 1969, Velma would drop a cigarette on the floor of her home and waited until her husband inhaled enough smoke to die.

His death, however, would do nothing to solve Velma's problems.

Her addictions and anxiety would only get worse.

A HOSPITAL FREQUENT FLYER

Velma would have another nervous breakdown after killing Thomas and lapse into a guilt-ridden depression. But seven months later, a co-worker at the Belk department store would introduce her to fifty-four-year-old Jennings Barfield. Jennings had emphysema and diabetes but Velma would marry him anyway. Unlike her marriage with Thomas which started out well, Velma's marriage with the older Jennings would be troubled from the start. Her drug addiction would escalate and Jennings would express his own regret at marrying her.

"I don't know why I married her," Jennings said. "All she does is pop pills all day."

After less than three years of marriage, Velma decided to part ways with Jennings. She didn't file for divorce, however, she decided to poison him with arsenic. She would later claim that she only meant to "make him sick."

Jennings Barfield was already ill and doctors had no suspicion that Velma was behind the death. Arsenic was a slow burn poison that could kill without detection. The autopsy called for no arsenic test and Velma had gotten away with murder once again.

But Seven months later, Velma would overdose on her prescription meds and become hospitalized. Her family recognized the pattern but could not wean Velma off of the drinks. She would remain hospitalized for three weeks.

Her personality seemed to change after the hospital release. She returned to work at Belk department store but kept being combative and argumentative with customers. Her boss knew of her circumstances and tried to coax her to do better. He took her away from the public contact and into the back stock room where he had her put pricing on the clothing items.

Her boss soon realized that Velma's addiction had gotten out of control. Velma would not be able to function in the back room, leaving tasks uncompleted as she would have her prescription medications delivered to the store.

"It is a hopeless situation," the store manager told Velma's son Ronnie before he fired his mother.

BROKE AND DESTITUTE

With no income, Velma would lose the family home as she no longer paid the mortgage. She would be forced to move back in with her parents and face the two people she blamed everything for.

Her father had grown ill, however, and would die from lung cancer shortly after Velma moved back into the home. She would feel bad about her father's death and admit that she had a love/hate relationship with him.

"I had learned to love him as much as I had hated him," Velma said. "He was so good to my kids. I think he tried to do with my kids like he wished he had done to us. He could not stand to see me correct them. If I would pick them up and spank them, he would ask me, 'Isn't that enough?'"

But after her father's death Velma self-medicated once again. She overdosed and was hospitalized for two weeks. Her family didn't judge, they instead thought she was "cursed."

"Velma needed psychiatric help," Orange said. "So she began medicating herself with deleterious results. She would "doctor shop" for different physicians who would be manipulated into giving her the drugs she wanted. Her addiction eventually grows until she becomes desperate for money in order to fuel the drug habit."

A MURDERER AND A THIEF

Velma began stealing from those closest to her, starting with her mother. Her mother confronted Velma about a missing check and Velma went ballistic.

"She had violent mood swings," Orange said. "The medication had completely changed her personality as she needed the drugs above all else. The people around her were not familiar with how to handle a person who had this kind of mental illness. So this made for a very dangerous cocktail for her and anyone close to her."

Hitting a new low, Velma took out a $1,000 loan under her mother Lillie's name. She put up the family home as collateral and forged her mother's signature on the documents. Velma then blew through the money and a month later took out another loan, once again using her mother's house as collateral. The following month, she emptied the checking account on her now deceased husband, Jennings. Two months later, the loan company began sending Velma overdue notices as she had not been paying off the loan.

"In Velma's mind," Orange said. "She had no other choice but to kill off her own mother."

Velma went to the local pharmacy and looked for bottles that had the warning of "fatal if ingested." She put the poison into a drink for her mother and watched as she drank the fatal elixir.

Her mother then began vomiting and lost control of her bowels. Within a few hours, her mother could not so much as walk and an ambulance was called.

Velma came to visit her in the hospital to finish the job. Armed with a Thermos, she made a special concoction of chicken soup and arsenic.

"Drink it slow," Velma said as she tenderly lifted the cups to the lips of her ailing mother. "Slow."

Her mother would eventually die of "natural causes" as no one suspected Velma of committing murder. Instead, she received sympathy.

"So sorry for your loss," hospital staff said.

"The thing with arsenic is that it shuts down the whole system," Orange said. "So hospital staff just chalked up her mother's weakness to old age. Checking for arsenic poisoning would be the furthest thing from their mind."

Velma showed the necessary emotion and received sympathy from friends and family. She then moved in with her daughter Kim and son-in-law Dennis who lived in a trailer park. She could not evade the authorities for long though as the authorities caught wind of Velma's check forgeries.

Velma reacted as she always did. She would run away and medicate herself.

"Her drug addiction kept pushing her into a corner and she saw no way out," Orange said. "So, this time, she goes to her son Ronnie's house and overdoses again, trying to kill herself. She falls and breaks her collar bone which laid her out in the hospital another three weeks."

But the police find her situation unsympathetic.

"We're sorry, Velma," the deputy informed her at her hospital bed. "But once you have been cleared for release, we will arrest you."

Velma would not have that. She tried to overdose again but this go around the hospital staff pumped out her stomach.

She was sent to court the next day and sentenced to six months in jail for the forgery. She is released after four months for good behavior.

NO REHAB HERE

Her addiction still unchecked, Velma returned to live with Kim and her son-in-law. She rummaged through the belongings of her son-in-law and stole a check, forging his name so she can get more prescription meds. Her daughter Kim now has caught wind of her mother's addiction, pleading with her doctors to stop prescribing her.

"In some ways," Orange said. "The doctors were just as guilty as she was. But back in the day, there was no way to cross-reference this stuff like we do now. Once she had her fill with one doctor she would go to the next and the next."

Velma's addiction prevented her from taking a forty-hour a week job. So she looked for alternative forms of income.

She would find a job taking care of the elderly.

Montgomery and Dolly Edwards would be her first clients.

"She found herself some easy targets," Orange said. "There didn't seem to be any legislative body in place that prevents sociopaths from caretaking the elderly. So Velma doesn't slip through any cracks, she just befriends the elderly couple and begins taking care of them."

Montgomery was blind and unable to walk. He was 93-years old and his 83-year old wife was too feeble to take care of him. They paid $75 a week for Velma to become their live-in caretaker.

All was good, at least in the beginning. But Dolly had a sharp tongue and would criticize Velma daily. Velma would keep a nice exterior unless confronted, saw Dolly has yet another wheel in her cycle of verbal abuse.

"It seemed to be a never-ending loop for her," Orange said. "Being forced to deal with verbally abusive people. Velma had long since snapped and Dollie simply had no idea who she was dealing with."

Velma began to plot out Montgomery and Dollie's demise until she meets their nephew, Stuart Taylor.

Stuart was already married but was blown away when he met the caretaker of his Aunt Dollie.

Velma would play it cool, stealing what she could from the couple in terms of petty cash and household items that had value. They outlived their usefulness to her within a year as Montgomery died of "natural causes". One month later, Dolly also passed away.

And again, no one suspected the sweet and soft-spoken Velma to have had anything to do with their deaths.

MOVING ON

Velma saw being a caretaker as a perfect front for her. She could steal as much money as she could and when the old folks detected something amiss she would simply poison them. After killing the Edwards' couple, she set the word out at church that she as available to be a caregiver. The pastor would refer her to Margie Lee Pittman who was seeking for a caregiver for her elderly parents, John Henry and Record Lee.

"She comes here twice a week," the pastor reassured Pittman. "She's a nice, kindly woman. You can't go wrong."

Pittman's father, John Henry Lee, was eighty years old when he discovered that his new caregiver had forged a $50 check on his account. He then fell violently ill, suffering through a spastic spell of vomiting, diarrhea, and convulsions. The doctors would chalk up his quick death to gastroenteritis but in fact, he had been poisoned with arsenic.

Velma played the caregiver role until his end. She attended his funeral and cried with the family, sending an ornate wreath (with money stolen from the dead man) to the proceedings.

For whatever reason, Velma spared Lee's wife and moved back to Lumberton, North Carolina to live in a trailer park. She began working as an aide in a nursing home and received word from Stuart that he was now a widow. The two began dating and she moved part of her belongings into his home.

"Stuart is a nice guy," Orange said. "He has no idea what kind of woman Velma is. She is so manipulative and cunning that the younger man is putty in her hands. So the relationship starts great as she reels him in with kindness and charm."

The couple are happy cohabitating until Stuart Stuart finds a letter addressed to Velma from the state penitentiary.

Curious, he began reading the correspondence and realized that is from a former cellmate of Velma.

Stuart became enraged. He threatened to "expose" Velma to all of his family and friends. Somehow, someway, however, she was able to calm him down.

He then found out that she had forged over $200 in checks on his account. The two argued but stayed together for the next two months.

"Velma had the Christian facade down pat," Orange said. "She asked Stuart to forgive her and the next thing you know they are going to a Rex Humbard revival. But before they went, she poured arsenic poison in both his beer and tea. She made sure he drank every drop."

Returning home from the revival, Stuart started to vomit on the drive home, the poison kicking in.

Velma had to keep the con going. She had to appear like a concerned girlfriend so she called up Stuart's daughter, Alice, later that night and told her that Stuart had came down with the flu.

Stuart's daughter expressed concern but Velma kept her at bay.

"Don't you worry now, honey. I'll take care of everything."

Stuart died the next day.

Velma would speak at Stuart's funeral and tearfully asked for his wedding band. His family graciously allowed her to have it and gave her $400 to help her cope with the grief.

But Alice knew her father was a picture of health. She vociferously argued for more tests beyond the standard autopsy and sure enough, arsenic had been found in Stuart's tissues.

On March 10th, 1978, the sheriffs arrived at Velma's home to bring her in for questioning. She was interrogated for over three hours, holding her ground. But she knows the evidence will trump her denials and tries to commit suicide after being released. This go around, however, her son Ronnie stopped her.

The sheriffs come to visit Velma again and she has one more surprise up her sleeve.

But Velma has one more surprise up her sleeve.

She would confess. Not only for the murder of Stuart but of six others.

"I set my first husband on fire," Velma confessed without an attorney present. "And I killed the rest of them."

"It was almost as if she wanted to be free of the guilt she had been carrying," Orange said. "Her confession seemed to take a burden off her back."

"The last ten years were like that," Velma said. "A drug nightmare. It was a case of not knowing where you are or what you've done."

The bodies of her victims were later exhumed and all tested positive for arsenic.

FACING THE GRIM REAPER

Velma's case would be prosecuted by Joe Freeman Britt, who was listed in the Guinness Book of World Records as the country's "deadliest prosecutor."

Velma would plead not guilty by reason of insanity but the court denied her plea.

"I needed to keep them sick until I could pay back the money I had stolen from them," Velma said. "I wanted to earn their thanks by nursing them back to health. I needed the money. I was addicted to pain killers. Anti-depressants. Amphetamines."

On November 23rd, 1978, Velma's trial would begin in Elizabethtown, North Carolina where she would be charged with the first-degree murder of her boyfriend, Stuart Taylor. The trial lasted seven days and the jury reached a verdict of guilty, placing her on death row at the age of 47. She was scheduled to be executed on February 3rd, 1979 but received a stay.

Velma would be sentenced to death and the verdict was appealed all the way to the U.S. Supreme court. Her attorney maintained that the jury had never been presented with the full extent of Velma's "addiction and background." Velma remained tight-lipped about that to everyone but her pastor. Her attorney felt thought her horrific background could have been used as part of her defense and the jury would have found her to be more of a sympathetic case.

CHANGING SPOTS?

"She's not the same person who went to prison in 1978," Kim Burke Norton, Velma's daughter said.

While in jail, Velma became a model prisoner.

"The first week I was here was the worst week," Velma recalled. "Everything about it."

Velma no longer had access to her drugs in prison and she began to dry out. With daily visits from two different pastors, Velma began to discuss her anger and repressed issues that fueled her addiction and murders.

Velma would claim that as she was awaiting trial in 1978 she came to a "meeting with Christ" that caused her to "change inwardly."

Velma heard a broadcast by radio evangelist JK Kinkle. "Jesus loves you, prisoners, too," Kinkle said. "He died for you too. No matter what you've done, the Lord will forgive you."

After Velma heard this sermon, she dropped to her knees and cried out to God.

She would then become the "go to" counselor for young inmates in the prison.

The inmates would nickname Velma as "Mama Margie" because of her wisdom and she would in turn think of them as her "adopted children."

The prison guards and counselors would take the most incorrigible prisoners and place them in a cell next to Velma. Velma would invariably counsel the young prisoner and advise them on the correct path.

"They'd come in ready to kill themselves," Sister Mary Teresa Floyd said. "And here she was with a death sentence, mothering and helping them."

"Living in prison is a struggle," Velma said. "Even at its best. And I know that without Him and His strength that has sustained me, I couldn't have made it even this far."

Her stay on death row soon became a part of the news brief. During this time, a phalanx of evangelists would take her cause to the mainstream. The Reverend Hugh Hoyle would become Velma's personal minister as she received stays of execution in September, October and December of 1981. She would also have a letter correspondence with Ruth Graham, Billy Graham's wife as well as meeting their daughter Ann.

While Velma impressed the Christian do-gooders, the family members of the victims were not taken in by her "conversion."

"She's got religion now, they say," Margie Lee Pittman said. "Well, she had religion before. So we all thought."

A few more stays were granted until 1984 when the U.S. Supreme Court justice Warren Burger granted her a stay until August of that year. At this point, however, her execution seemed inevitable. In an ironic move, Velma would choose poison rather than the gas chamber and enjoyed the final visits from her children and grandchildren.

During the final week before her execution, the Reverend Hoyle, and his wife came to the prison with a battery-powered portable keyboard. His wife played the little organ then the Reverend sang "He Hideth My Soul" and "He is So precious to Me" in the cramped visitor booth.

Velma sang along, whistling in the graveyard before the reaper came for her.

She then wrote letters to each of the victim's family asking them for forgiveness. Reverend Hoyle would deliver the letters to the families, all of whom would refuse them.

MEET THE HANGMAN

As her execution date neared, Velma was placed in a solitary cell that stood directly across from the death chamber.

"It's total isolation," Velma said. "From everyone I had been with for six years."

North Carolina Governor James B.Hunt would reject her final plea for clemency.

On the day of her execution, the jail house would turn into a media frenzy. Death penalty advocates gathered outside the prison and chanted "Hip, hip, hurrah...K-I-L-L" while some sloganeered with "burn, bitch, burn". The protesters held up a few placards that quote Romans ch.13 which ironically was a verse that Velma would repeat to guards during her prison stay.

"For rulers are not a terror to good works, but to the evil...(The ruler) beareth no the sword in vain, for he is the minister of God, a revenger to execute wrath upon him that doeth evil."

The execution was scheduled to take place at 2:00 a.m but the protesters remained outside, their chants reduced to a simple "Kill her! Kill her!"

On November 2nd, 1984, Velma would be executed by lethal injection. The prison official came out and addressed the press, giving out copies of Barfield's statement of apology. The reporters then eagerly anticipated what Velma requested for her last meal. Initially, Velma just wanted the normally scheduled prison food; chicken livers, collard greens and a sheet cake with peanut butter icing. The last meal was delivered but Velma immediately lost her appetite. Instead, she opted for Cheese Doodles and a glass of Coca-Cola.

"Her attorney believed that Velma could have done some good in life," Orange said. "He stated that she could have become a teacher, counselor or a pastor. But her father set her on a path of self-destruction that she couldn't escape from. By the time she the left that road to ruin, she was too far gone in terms of her murderous acts. Justice had to be served in the end. In the end, the law doesn't care how genuine you are in your pleas for forgiveness. It only cares about the rule of law."

"I'm sorry for the hurt that I've caused," Velma said before her execution. "So many people, today if it were possible, I wish I could take every bit of hurt on myself."

GOD TOLD ME TO: THE TRUE STORY OF GWEN HENDRICKS

Gwen Gillespie Hendricks was born into a Navy family in Memphis, Tennessee in 1955.

Her father was a naval officer while her mother was a housewife. Like most military families, they moved often from station to station, according to her father's assignment. Growing up in a devoutly Catholic home and Gwen would embrace the religion with fervor.

Gwen dressed with modesty, wearing button down shirts and minimal make-up. She fostered a nerd look, with wire-rimmed glasses and short hair.

Carrying on the family's military tradition, she joined the Air Force at the age of twenty-five. It was there she would meet Jim Hendricks, twenty-four, who was her instructor.

Jim Hendricks was a tall, strapping Air Force sergeant with an air of authority. He had an easy smile and Gwen found him easy on the eyes.

"Well, it was kind of instant attraction," Gwen recalled. "There was a bit of lust there as he's a very tall, handsome man. The Air Force can tell you that you can't date but they can't tell you who to marry so I went to the Jag office and asked if I could marry my STA and they said 'yes.'"

The two were married in 1980. Jim had a five year old daughter, Season Hendricks, from a previous relationship. In 1982, they would have a son, Ben.

Because of their career choice, the couple spent a lot of time apart during the early years of their marriage. Jim was stationed at Wake Island while Gwen was assigned to Eglin Air Force Base in Florida.

The couple would be reunited in 1986 as Jim was assigned to the Air Force Academy in Colorado Springs. Gwen would not re-enlist in the Air Force, instead taking a job with the Internal Revenue Service.

The couple spent three years in Colorado before Jim would be transferred to Guam in August of 1989. He took the the entire family with him to the island.

"I figured we had a pretty normal family," Season said. "Until we moved to Guam. Things started to change. She (Gwen) would pick fights. She was jealous of the time my Dad and I would spend together."

"She (Gwen) had a different life in mind for herself," forensic psychologist Joyce Smith said. "She was used to having her own money. So when they moved to Guam there was little to do and less money to do it with."

Gwen and the children moved back to the United States, returning to Colorado and leaving Jim in Guam.

She would buy a home in Littleton and once again start working for the IRS. She then joined the junior Chamber of Commerce where she met Terry Knaack and a woman named Rochelle.

"Rochelle was into tarot cards," Gwen said. "And Terry was into new age occultism. My religion, my faith was still very meaningful to me. I wanted to do Bible study with them to get them out of what I considered witchcraft. Rochelle said she wouldn't go to Bible study with me unless I did the cards with her and the same with Terry. So I think I opened up the door to hell. Right after I started, everything went wrong"

During this time, Gwen began to experience health issues. She suffered from dizzy spells and nausea.

Her personality shifted as well, changing from being even-tempered to easily agitated and manic. With her health and ability to focus effected, Gwen stepped down from her revenue collector position to tax examiner.

"Could the illness have played a part in her deciding to kill her husband?" Smith asked. "Maybe. But Gwen was really steeped into religion and sounded like she embraced some of the more fringe elements of Christianity. She truly believed that occultism was a form of witchcraft and that those things could do her harm. So when she suffered from her illness she erroneously attributed it to her dabbling in the occult. She was a woman who preferred supernatural explanations to rational thought."

Gwen also started to grow deeper into debt, buying expensive gifts for friends.

In the fall of 1990, Gwen hired Terry Knaack to help remodel the Littleton home. A few months later, Knaack moved into the couple's basement with the rationale being he would be able to help with the mortgage. With the husband away and a man in the home, Gwen began to fantasize about Terry and starting over with him.

"Terry would talk a lot about wanting to having a ranch for children with special needs," Gwen recalled. "And I started having delusions that he and I would start this ranch together for the children."

"She entered into a fantasy world," Smith said. "She began imagining a life with this other man, having delusions of grandeur of what they would do together. He became her willing accomplice in her dreams, since her own husband was absent because of military duty. So an alternate universe with Terry Knaack became her obsession. What probably started as harmless day dreams soon grew into something sinister."

"I also believe that Gwen had more than a little bit of a Messiah complex. She had this compulsion to save people and it manifested in doling out gifts and handouts to people who she felt were in need. She had this secret life and kept things from Jim who was away on military assignment. Those secrets involved getting into credit card debt."

By January of 1991, Gwen began telling friends that she was having premonitions of Jim dying in a plane crash.

"I had this really bad dream over and over again," Gwen recalled. "Where Jim had died in a plane crash. I was thinking, well after Jim died that I would marry Terry and we'd start this ranch but of course Terry didn't know anything about because it was all in my head."

Gwen then began hearing voices.

"They (the voices) wanted me to sacrifice what was most dear in my life," Gwen recalled. "I remember thinking that I have to answer these voices because this is coming from God. You know, I've got to sacrifice what I loved the most and that was Jim."

Gwen kept a journal where she logged the "premonitions" of her husband's death. She titled the journal "The Courage to Will and Persevere," She described the voices that she heard and believed that God had told her to kill Jim.

"She experienced what we call 'command hallucinations,'" said Smith. "These are sometimes coupled with someone's value system, in this case, it was Gwen's religion. Gwen believed that she should obey God and believed that the voices that she heard were, in fact, coming from God. So this could go bad real quick if those voices told her to do damage to someone."

"She was past the breaking point, a delusional schizophrenic that was not diagnosed. When she confided with friends it was probably with people who shared her same point of view, people who believed in visions, messages from God and premonitions. Gwen was a soft-spoken woman and even if someone thought she was crazy they would not think she would be capable of taking a gun and blowing someone's brains out. She didn't have that violent vibe."

But behind closed doors, Gwen would deal with problems or difficulties in a haphazard fashion. She would often open up the Bible and believed that whatever random verse she came upon was a direct message from God.

"I reread Psalm 90 quite a few times before a small voice said, 'Keep reading, keep reading.'" Gwen wrote in her journal. "After reading the first page of stanzas, I knew I would be protected from the car bombs, the knifings, the guns, the contracts and all the other evil I had seen connected with busting the pornographers and pimps. Those mafia guys play rough, but somehow they just won't be able to get me. Then I turned the page to continue reading. It felt like a giant fist had slammed into my heart. I literally could not breath [sic]. I burst into sobs and sunk to the floor. I cried for Jim because he really was going to die."

Gwen began to prepare for Jim's death, taking out a $300,000 life insurance policy on her husband payable on his death.

She then visited a local banker, informing him that she would be soon be receiving proceeds from insurance claim. Gwen was told that she would not be able to use the money as long as Jim was alive. She then forged a doctor's note which alleged that she had multiple sclerosis. She submitted this note to the Red Cross along with a letter stating that they should be responsible for being her husband back from Guam.

Gwen did not want the proceeds from the insurance for her own material gain. She believed that she could use the proceeds from his life insurance to establish the "James Hendricks Foundation" to aid victims of mafia produced pornography.

"She became obsessed with pornographers," Smith said. "Like most people with Messiah Complexes, she chose an ill of society and focused on that, believing that she was a chosen vessel to help eradicate the 'sin'. In her deluded mind, she needed this money to accommodate

God's will to establish this ranch wherein she would save victims of pornography. The only way she could attain this goal would be to kill Jim and take the life insurance proceeds."

"I was very desperate to have him (Jim) back," Gwen said. "I felt like I was at my limit and not really realizing that I actually was really having a breakdown."

With her husband not even dead yet, Gwen began purchasing clothes for herself and the children to wear for his funeral.

She bought silk flowers and boxes of Kleenex for mourning friends and family.

Gwen also increased the amount of Jim's life insurance from $300,000 to $1,000,000.

True to her premonition, she bought a wedding dress for herself and put a wedding ring on layaway for Knaack.

Gwen would ask God to speak to her directly and "guide her hand" as she thumbed through her Bible. When she got to a passage, she would believe that was what God wanted her to study."

"For the first reading, only the last sentence made sense," Gwen wrote. *"I had asked if what I felt about Jim's death was real. He said yes.*

God can even speak through the dictionary!

After reading the first page of stanzas, I knew I would be protected from car bombs, the knifings, the guns, the contracts and all the other evil I had seen connected with busting pornographers and pimps. Those Mafia guys play rough, but somehow they just won't be able to get me."

"You can see her delusions of grandeur in her journal writings," Smith said. "She had all of the symptoms of a delusional narcissist, truly believing that God made her as the 'Chosen One.'"

Gwen would write that she had a two-way conversation with God about creating the ranch.

"'Oh, so the ranch is in Douglas county near to the Springs so my family will be protected from the mafia guys' Then I knew in Denver, I'm Gwen Hendricks. In the Springs, I'm Gwen Knaack. I had thought the clinic would carry the name of the ranch, but with this new insight, I knew that for safety sake, everything had to be kept separate."

She continued to have health issues as well, as the nausea and attacks of dizziness still had not subsided. Physicians could not determine the cause of her illness. She was eventually diagnosed with Ménière's disease, an ailment that causes vertigo and a fluctuating hearing loss. She had a micro-shunt placed into her ear which only helped relieve the pain she was experiencing.

Her mental health, however, continued to deteriorate.

Jim would return to Colorado for good in May of 1991. It would not be a well-received reunion, however, as the couple fought over everything specifically the living arrangements of Knaack. Jim promptly kicked the boarder out of the home.

He then took control of the finances as he discovered that Gwen had maxed out the credit cards.

"My brother said that she had apparently taken several other credit cards and had maxed them out to the limit," recalled Steve Hendricks, Jim's brother. "And he was furious with her at that point. He did confide in me that he was thinking about leaving Gwen."

Jim would take away all of Gwen's credit cards and this made her extremely angry.

"He took away her power," Smith said. "She got an ego boost by buying expensive gifts for friends and helping out women that she thought were in need. When Jim took that away, she saw him as someone who needed to be eliminated."

Divorce seemed imminent but Gwen seemed immune to it all in her journal writings.

"The funeral, the ranch school, children, the foundation, always being pushed forward," she wrote. "I have to do what I have to do, too. But just for now I'm going to take one day at a time. I'm hoping I don't get too compulsed to do anything more for at least this coming week. I need to rest.

Perhaps I should start by explaining the little voice. It's my voice, but not me. It comes from somewhere inside, and if I don't listen to it, act on it, it becomes a compulsion. If I don't listen and act on the compulsion, it grows stronger and stronger until it dominates all aspects of my life. I learned long ago to listen and do what I'm told. Things work out when I do, and when I don't, things get real miserable...Yes, my little voice is the way God reaches me with the Holy Spirit."

With Jim now home on a permanent basis, The voices in her head grew louder. They began to speak with more urgency in telling her that she had to kill her husband.

"True to her religious background, she did not interpret auditory hallucinations as a sign of mental illness," Smith said. "Gwen was the kind of woman who took the stories in the Bible literally, seeing herself as a modern day Abraham who heard voices from God. You hear it in the way she describes the voices in her head telling her to sacrifice her husband in the same way the Bible speaks of God telling Abraham to sacrifice his son Isaac."

"I said 'Lord I surrender to you,'" Gwen recalled. "I'm hearing voices from God and this is what God wants and I have to get this from God and if this is what God wants then I have to give it to him. So I went out and I bought a gun"

"The voices in her head told her it was time," Smith said. "And true to her value system, she had to obey. For her religion was not a therapeutic aid because of the way she had viewed it. Her God was a vengeful one, a violent one."

On Friday, August 17th, 1991 Gwen drove to Peterson Air Force Base to meet with her husband, a 75 mile drive, to bring him a change of clothes.

"Jim was working late and he asked me to bring him something to eat." Gwen said.

She had informed police that Jim was working all night to prepare for an inspection but changed his mind.

Gwen wrote in her journal about the incident.

When Jim called to say he was on his way home, I went into shock. I knew the time was at hand. I knew I wasn't really ready. I screamed and cried and raged. Then I asked again, if he was meant to die or was I just suckered into some kind of head game. Benjamin's daddy died. I cried myself to sleep that night. I thought what was I supposed to do with two husbands. God has the oddest sense of humor."

"She told me that she was gonna make a nice little picnic for them," Gwen's step-daughter Season recalled. "They were going to make a night of it and that she wanted him to feel good for his inspection."

Gwen left the home and dropped off both Season and son Ben with a friend. When Gwen arrived at the Air Force base, however, she stated that Jim told her that he was heading home. She maintained that the two then went back home in separate cars.

"His truck was in the lead," Gwen said. "I was in the car behind. I remember being so tired, I told him I can't go on anymore. I just want a quick nap and let's get in the back of the truck."

She said that they traveled in separate cars but she became tired and slept through the night at a rest stop along Interstate 25.

Police, however, believed that Gwen lured Jim to an abandoned stretch of highway with the promise of sex.

The two met at the side of the road and Gwen hesitated when thinking of pulling out the gun. She wanted her husband to go peacefully.

"I took the gun out from underneath the seat of the car," Gwen said. "I got into the truck and laid next to him and when I could feel that he was deeply sleeping that's when I shot him."

Gwen would shoot Jim six times.

"It was like I was outside of myself," Gwen said. "Looking and watching what I was doing. I felt very numb, very cold, like I was on auto-pilot. I got back into my car and I took apart the gun and I was just throwing the parts out the window and just driving around, just in a fog, not knowing what I was doing, where I was going. I stopped at a roadside rest stop. Fell asleep. When I woke up and I didn't know everything that happened."

When Gwen arrived back home that Saturday she began making calls to the police, stating that her husband was missing.

On Monday morning, she called Jim's supervisor who sent out two officers to search for him.

One of his co-workers would find his pickup truck on the side of Highway 83 in Douglas County. His body had been placed in the camper shell in back of his truck.

He had been shot six times in the chest and neck with a small caliber handgun.

Gwen would become the primary suspect.

Police noted that she hardly showed any emotion when they informed her of her husband's death.

"Her state of mind was that of a wife with a missing husband," one of the deputies recalled. "When she was telling a story, she couldn't stick with the same story. And that's a clue, obviously, to law enforcement."

Gwen would then break the news to Jim's daughter, Season.

"Gwen said they found him by the side of the road in his car," Season said. "And that he had been murdered. I don't remember her crying. It was the worst moment of my life."

Terry Knaack would be helpful in the case against Gwen. She had been secretly in love with him and given him her diary. He read through her writings and promptly delivered the diary to the Douglas County Sheriff's Department. The sheriffs then instructed him to call Gwen while they would listen in.

Gwen would tell Knaack that she didn't kill Jim but that she wanted to die. Then Douglas County Sheriff's Department Kim Castellano's intuition told her something was wrong. The Hendricks had two pre-teens, a boy and a girl and the boy was never around during questioning.

Castellano believed that Gwen had a problem with males. With one of the male investigators, an Air Force official, by her side, Castellano went back to talk to Gwen.

Once again, the boy was not there. Gwen was overly polite to Castellano, asking her if she wanted anything to eat and jumping up to fix her something before she could answer.

Gwen would totally ignored the male detective.

Castellano used this knowledge to her advantage and befriended Gwen, sensing that the delusional woman would be much more forthcoming with a female officer than a male.

Gwen began trusting her enough that she asked for Castellano's help in balancing her check book. The detective then saw that Hendricks had recently taken out several insurance policies that would be hers when her husband died.

The investigators then used a technique police refer to as the "midnight confession." Castellano and the Air Force official went over to the Hendricks house at eleven at night, waking Gwen up.

Questioning her in the family room, Gwen continued to deny her involvement in her husband's killing. Castellano and her partner then took turns reading from Gwen's journal, tightening the screws on her denial. They also saw Jim's watch on the counter.

Castellano then told her to get dressed and that she was being taken in.

Gwen finally cracked. She curled into a fetal position and confessed.

"Two stories that night—the story of the rest area and the story of Highway 83," she sobbed.

Gwen would go on to describe the highway story.

"There is blood everywhere, I can see it everywhere," she said. "It's terrible. My mind won't let me remember. I don't know if I shot him or not. I don't know what's real anymore."

Gwen was then taken to a local hospital where she stayed for two days for a mental health evaluation. She was arrested upon release and charged with her husband's murder.

After undergoing another mental health examination, Gwen was deemed delusional but understood the charges being levied against her.

Because of this, she was found fit to stand trial.

In court, however, Gwen continued to state that she didn't kill her husband. She said that the body found at the crime scene was not Jim's.

"There was the obvious choice for her attorneys to declare her insane," Smith said. "She had one hell of an imagination and could make things up on the fly. She said during the trial that she became completely convinced that her husband was still alive, going into full blown denial. 'He's still alive, he's out there somewhere and you have to find him', she would say. She was completely delusional."

Her first attorney, Lloyd Boyer, stated that it was physically impossible for Gwen to have murdered Jim Hendricks.

"The lack of gunshot residue inside the Capitol (Jim's car) vehicle," Boyer said. "Indicated that the murder had not occurred in the vehicle. Mr. Hendricks was quite a bit larger than Gwen and she was small, not especially strong and could not have moved the victim into the vehicle."

The investigators failed to produce the gun that Gwen used but the prosecution had another tool at its disposal.

The first link was Jim's watch that they found in Gwen's possession, which showed that she had tampered with the crime scene. The prosecution showed how she was going to use the money from the insurance policies and start a "home for troubled people" that would be near the spot where she killed her husband.

The jury found her guilty of first-degree murder and Hendricks was sentenced to life in prison.

"I just kept my faith that Jim would come rescue me and I would be set free from prison," Gwen said. "Of course, that never happened."

Inside the prison, physicians deemed her to be mentally unfit to be included with the general population and transferred her to the psychiatric unit.

"They got me on anti-psychotics," Gwen said. "And anti-depressants but it wasn't until 1997 that I started having memories of what had happened. At first, it was like just pictures and they hit me like bricks, you know. I killed a great husband and Dad. I robbed Season and Ben of their father. I felt lower than dirt."

She did have help, however, as some legal advocates filed briefs on her behalf, claiming that she had been insane at the time of her trial.

In September of 2000, the Supreme Court of Colorado overturned Gwen's conviction and ordered a new trial.

In April of 2001, a judge ruled that Gwen was not guilty by reason of insanity.

The trial lasted ten minutes.

"She came to terms with what she had done," Smith said. "She had stopped protesting, stop denying and admitted to what she had done."

Gwen was then remanded to a psychiatric care facility in Colorado. She then decided to change her name to "Emi Masai".

"When I lost Jim," Gwen said. "I also lost my children. I longed to be a wife and mother again. I redefined myself as married to Christ and being a mother to all the people I meet."

"By renaming herself she thought that she could obtain a new identity," Smith said. "It was a way of divorcing herself from her past transgressions."

Gwen went through four years of psychiatric treatment where the physicians determined that she was no longer a threat to society. She was released to a residential program where she now helps the needy at Mercy Ministries.

She continues to take her anti-psychotic medication.

"I never want to slip back into mental illness again," Gwen said. "I literally thank God every morning I open my medicine cabinet. I've always said justice wasn't done. Justice in this case would have been my execution. A life for a life. But it's not about fairness. It's about recognizing mental illness and knowing that you're not responsible for what you are doing when you're psychotic."

Gwen has had minimal contact with both her son and step-daughter since she committed the murder of their father.

"I long to see them but they let it be known through family channels that they don't want to see me," Gwen said. "So I respect that."

"I'm really glad that Gwen has helped herself enough to admit what she's done," Season said. "And I hope there never is a time where it gets easy for her to look in the mirror. Because there's never a time where it's easy to be without our Dad."

"I wish I could take it back," Gwen said. "Be a good wife and Mom again. I can't turn the clock back. So all I can do is give them my deepest apology and ask them to forgive me."